HANS UNGER

Practical Mosaics

STUDIO VISTA

Dedication

To Eberhard Schulze

in memory of all the mosaics we scrapped while learning our craft

Acknowledgements

The author and publishers are grateful to the following artists for permission to reproduce their work: Joseph Young (Plate 25), Antony Hollaway (Plates 26 & 27), Robert Stewart (Plate 30), Juan O'Gorman (Plates 31 & 32), José Chávez Morado (Plate 34), Jeanne Reynal (Plate 35); and to the following photographers: Colorphoto Hinz, Basle (Plates 1, 13 & 14), Alinari/Mansell (Plate 9), Anderson/Mansell (Plates 12 & 15), J. W. Hersee (Plate 16), U. Trapani, Ravenna (Plate 19), Giraudon (Plate 20), Marvin Rand (Plates 31 & 32), Eberhard Schulze (Plate 36).

Also to J. M. Meulenhoff, Amsterdam, for Plates 2, 5, 6, 7 & 10; the Trustees of the British Museum for Plate 3; Museo Nazionale, Naples, for Plate 4; Messrs L. A. G. Prichard Son & Partners, Liverpool, for Plate 8; Musei Capitolini, Rome, for Plate 11; the Swedish Institute for Cultural Relations for Plate 17; Kunstgewerbemuseum, Zurich for Plate 19; Musée Fernand Léger, Biot, for Plate 21; UNESCO, Paris, for Plate 22; Messrs Everett, Morgan & Grundy, London, for Plate 23; H. Owen Jones, London, for Plate 24; Richard J. Neutra & Robert Alexander, for Plate 25; Ambassador Publishing Company, London, for Plate 27; Carter Tiles Limited for Plate 28.

Plate 20 is © SPADEM, Paris, 1965. Plate 18 is taken from *Antoni Gaudí* by J. J. Sweeney, published by Verlag Gerd Hatje, Stuttgart; and Plate 35 from *The Mosaics of Jeanne Reynal*, published by Wittenborn and Company, New York (Collection Mrs David Metzger).

© Hans Unger 1965
Reprinted 1968

Published in Great Britain by Studio Vista Limited
Blue Star House, Highgate Hill, London N 19
Set in 11pt Plantin, 2pt leaded
Printed in Great Britain by Staples Printers Limited
at their Rochester, Kent, establishment

SBN 289 27990 9

Contents

List of Plates

1 History

A mosaic can be broadly defined as a unified composition created by assembling separate pieces of material. In this book we are mainly concerned with mosaics in which multi-coloured materials such as glass, marble, stone, etc., have been put together to form a pictorial whole. Seen from close to, a mosaic seems to be a random collection of units of material, but when it is viewed from the correct distance the eye of the beholder transforms the seemingly fortuitously arranged parts into a meaningful whole; he does, however, remain aware of the individual units of which the mosaic is composed. There have been periods in the history of the mosaic when mosaicists aimed at eliminating the separateness of the parts by using the tiniest stones set close together and giving the surface a high-gloss polish. Vasari, the Renaissance writer on art, actually describes the ideal mosaic as being indistinguishable from a painting. But this attitude invariably resulted in a decline of the mosaic as a creative art form. There is no doubt that one of the reasons for the special appeal of the mosaic is that the viewer unconsciously takes an active part in the creation of the unified picture. In this respect the mosaic technique is similar to the Pointillism of the nineteenth century; painters like Seurat built up their pictures by setting little daubs of pure colour next to each other; they thereby achieved effects of light and colour which could not be accomplished by mixing pigments on the palette in the ordinary way.

Mosaic making is a creative activity as ancient as art itself and mosaics dating back as far as the fourth millennium B.C. have been found in Mesopotamia. Both the Babylonians and the Egyptians decorated the walls and columns of their buildings with mosaics. But the direct roots of the art form which culminated in the gorgeous Byzantine creations of the early Christian era go back to the humble pebble mosaic floors of the Aegean area in the Eastern Mediterranean. From the beginning of the Greek civilization to the end of the Roman Empire mosaics were a widespread and popular form of floor decoration and a great number of them have been uncovered.

The early Greek mosaics were always made of uncut pebbles and, in the beginning, the designs consisted mainly of simple geometric patterns. Over the centuries the designs became more elaborate, but it must be admitted that the art of the mosaic never reached the heights of classical Greek sculpture and painting with which it was contemporaneous. The painting of the time clearly influenced the mosaic: the subjects of both art forms are chiefly mythological, or else consist of decorative animal and flower compositions. The treatment of the human figure in mosaic is reminiscent of the vase decorations of the time. 'Huntsman' (Plate 2), dating from about 350 B.C. and found in Pella in Macedonia, is a typical, simplified design with few gradations of light and shade; the light-coloured figure is set against a strongly contrasting dark background and the few details are drawn in simple lines.

True tesserae, i.e. small cubes cut from stone, marble and occasionally glass, were first introduced from the East at the time of Alexander the Great, about the middle of the fourth century B.C. This was a major step forward in the development of the mosaic: cut cubes with straight sides can be set closer together than the natural, rounded pebbles which had been used exclusively up to that time. This enabled the artists to give their work a degree of detail and refinement previously impossible. We can trace an ever-increasing refinement from the simple Greek mosaics of the fourth century B.C. to the elaborate Roman mosaics of the time of the birth of Christ.

Mosaic was the usual floor covering in the houses of the upper classes in the late Roman Empire. The innumerable mosaics uncovered in Roman villas as far apart as Britain and North Africa can still be seen today: in York, Cirencester, Woodchester, Brading on the Isle of Wight, to mention but a few which have been found in England; in Nenning near Trier in Germany; in Rheims, Aix-en-Provence, Lyons and St Colombe near Vienne in France; all along the North African coast, with especially well-preserved examples in Carthage such as the 'Head of a Sea God' (Plate 3). But the most sophisticated creations have been found in the affluent centres of Rome itself and Pompeii. Technical skill reached quite astonishing heights and artists began to work from paintings, creating 'paintings in stone' in which every nuance of shading, even the brush strokes, could be reproduced. These mosaics have, incidentally, been an invaluable source of our knowledge of classical painting, since the durable mosaic copies have outlived the more perishable originals. Realistic, three-dimensional paintings of scenes from mythology and the theatre, and even portraits of Roman society women were copied in mosaic. Plate 4 shows the high degree of refined realism that the mosaicists of the first century B.C. achieved. It was probably executed by a Greek craftsman who travelled to various cities of the Empire to carry out freelance commissions for mosaics. The stones he used are quite tiny so that such details as the high-lights on the lips and nose could be placed quite accurately. The soft gradation of the colour shades gives the whole portrait a three-dimensional effect and the expression is as life-like as a photograph.

The skill and patience which must have gone into the more elaborate mosaics of the time is astonishing: the famous Alexander mosaic of which we show a detail in Plate 5 was found in Pompeii; the whole mosaic is composed of an estimated one million tiny tesserae. Although the mosaic was created in 90 B.C., it is based on an earlier Greek painting done in the fourth century B.C., shortly after the battle of Issus which it depicts. The original painting must have been exceptionally lively and dramatic; the mosaicist has reproduced the vividness of the scene with superb skill. He has used only five basic colours: red, brown, yellow, black and white, and this limited 'palette' gives the whole composition a striking unity. The stones are set in serpentine lines which enabled the artist to follow the lively movement of each detail (e.g. the horse's tail). He thereby succeeded in reproducing the dramatic vigour of the battle; even though the mosaic is a close copy of the original painting, the mosaicist must have been a creative craftsman of outstanding skill.

At the same time as these realistic three-dimensional copies of paintings, quite a different style of mosaic was also popular, a style whose simplicity is reminiscent of the early Greek pebble mosaics. The mosaics in this style were executed in two or three colours only, often just in black and white; the subject matter was depicted in its simplest form, perspective was ignored and the human or animal figures were two-dimensional stylized silhouettes rather than realistic representations of nature. If I have called the realism of some mosaics almost photographic, the stylization in this type of mosaic recalls the modern poster in its striking simplicity. The famous 'Cave Canem' mosaic (Plate 6) is executed in three colours only: a black dog is set on a white background with the bright red tongue and leash as the only spots of colour. There is no attempt at realistic modelling; the treatment is entirely flat with a line here and there to clarify the form of the body. The rows of tesserae, both on the animal and on the background, define the form and movement in a manner which is characteristic for the mosaic medium as handled by an expert. We can still see today how the mosaicist first started with the outline of the animal's body; following the movement of the contours with the tesserae he gave definition to the form and only afterwards filled in the whole area.

These two different styles of mosaic flourished simultaneously: on the one hand the realistic copies of paintings, and on the other the simplified, stylized designs. The first was the translation of one medium (paint) into a fundamentally alien one (mosaic tesserae). Although this was frequently done with consummate skill and even virtuosity, it must be considered a misuse and debasement of the medium. Unlike paint, a severe material like a cube of stone does not lend itself to the creation of soft realistic effects and chiaroscuro. If this is attempted, the result is often curiously slick and lifeless as in the example reproduced in Plate 7, another mosaic from Pompeii. This shows the beginning of degeneration of the mosaic from a creative art form to a mere imitative craft, although the technical skill is of the highest order. A similar stylistic development at the beginning of the Renaissance and again during the nineteenth century was an important cause of the complete decline of the mosaic: during those periods the making of mosaics consisted of nothing more than a sterile copying process which could not develop further but only increase in technical virtuosity. On the other hand, when the natural limitations of the tesserae as a material are accepted and when their unique quality is used creatively to develop a suitable style, a style of simplification, monumental stylization or abstraction, the result can be artistically highly satisfying, as proved by many modern mosaics, or it can produce glorious works of art as it did during the great Byzantine periods. This problem of interrelation of design and material is of fundamental importance and every mosaicist has to come to terms with it. We will meet it again when discussing designing for mosaic (Chapter 4).

The materials used by mosaicists in Roman and Greek times were usually stone or marble tesserae. Glass cubes were also used occasionally, but at that time only a few colours in glass could be produced. The tesserae were set into a mortar of lime and pounded brick which was mixed with water. Sometimes volcanic ash known as 'Pozzolana' was used, a substance which has many of the properties of Portland cement. The design was scratched into the mortar and when the tesserae had been laid the crevices between them were filled ('grouted') with a mixture of lime and pounded white marble. Finally, the whole floor was polished until the surface became smooth. One can study a number of Roman mosaics in the British Museum and the Victoria and Albert Museum. Plate 3 shows a decorative mosaic of the head of a sea god at the British Museum; it was found in Carthage and dates from A.D. 200

By the fourth century A.D. Christianity had spread throughout the whole of the Roman Empire, and the Emperor Constantine the Great transferred the Imperial court from Rome to Byzantium, which was renamed Constantinople. During the following centuries the centre of religion and civilization shifted from the Western Latin to the Eastern Greek part of the Roman Empire, which became known as the Byzantine Empire.

These events had a tremendous influence on the development of the mosaic, especially since they coincided with two important technical developments: skill in glass-making improved greatly, and the technique of making gold tesserae was imported from Egypt. Within a short time glass tesserae with their greater brilliance and variety of colour almost completely replaced marble and stone tesserae. In addition the perfection of a light but strong mortar enabled the early Christian craftsmen to decorate not only floors but also walls and ceilings with mosaics. This development was not merely a technical advance in mosaic making: the raising of the mosaic from the floor to the walls and ceiling of the church is a physical expression of the rise of the mosaic from a merely decorative to a spiritual art. Soon it was to become the most characteristic form of Byzantine art. It was important for the early Christian Church to explain the new religion to the faithful by depicting scenes from the Old Testament and the life of Christ, and at the same time to overawe the spectator with the splendour of the House of God. The dogma of the Eastern Orthodox Church forbade any form of idolatry and therefore encouraged the creation of flat wall mosaics in preference to sculpture. In addition to these spiritual demands and to the technical advances in the field of glass and mortar, the architectural development also acted as a stimulus to mosaic making: the many arches, domes, vaults and apses in the new churches cried out for decoration and the bright but opaque glass tesserae were ideally suited to give an exciting surface texture to the walls whilst preserving their solidity.

The term Byzantine is not confined to the art of Byzantium itself but includes all those works created over a wide area whose spiritual sources spring from the civilization of the Byzantine, i.e. Eastern Roman, Empire. This civilization covered at one time or another the Balkans and Asia Minor, the Middle East and a good deal of the Italian peninsula and Sicily. Byzantine mosaics were created in places as far apart as Southern Russia and Spain.

The essence of Byzantine art lies in the fusion of Western and Eastern concepts: the transfer of the Imperial Court from Rome brought the classical ideals of beauty and realism to Constantinople. The influence of the East on art paralleled its influence on the religious thought of early Christianity: religious art had to express the new conception of the divine in its deep and awe-inspiring significance. We can trace this gradual fusion of East and West through the approximately 1,000 years of Byzantine art; the early mosaics are still largely classical in concept and, under the influence of Eastern ideas, the shift of emphasis is clearly towards the spiritual meaning of the religious figures.

Today the greatest number of the best-preserved Byzantine mosaics of the early period can be seen in Salonika and Ravenna. Ravenna had been an Imperial residence of both the Western and Eastern Empires at various times and lavish palaces and churches were built there. One of the oldest and artistically perhaps the most satisfying of the Ravenna chapels is the Mausoleum of Galla Placidia, built in the fifth century A.D. A classical calm pervades the mosaic of 'The Good Shepherd amongst his flock' (Plate 12). Roman paintings of emperors and figures from classical mythology clearly influenced the artist who created the idealized beardless figure of Christ who tends his flock in majestic splendour. This feeling of imperial nobility is emphasized by the lavish use of gold in Christ's garment and a large halo which is set against the soft blues and greens of the sky and landscape. On the other hand, the mosaics in the same chapel showing the Apostles in their white robes appearing from a dark blue background, the gently glowing night sky of the cupola with shimmering stars, the whole atmosphere of the interior in its rich mysterious luminosity and extraordinarily moving, dream-like quality, are far removed from the classical ideals of beauty or the idealistic representation of the Roman mosaics.

It is interesting to compare mosaics depicting an identical subject; they show clearly the different stylistic approaches of the Roman and Byzantine artists: 'Doves drinking from the Goblet of Faith' in the Ravenna Mausoleum of Galla Placidia (Plate 9), 'Doves of Pliny' from the Villa Hadrian, Tivoli, Rome (Plate 11) and 'Doves round a basin' from the House of the Faunus in Pompeii (Plate 10). The similarity of Plates 9 and 11 is such that one must suppose that the Byzantine artist was familiar with the Roman mosaic; note especially the position of the dove on the left of each mosaic. The Roman mosaic is a realistic genre picture; the plumage is shown in great detail, every individual feather is 'painted' in its true colour and one of the doves is busy preening itself. The Ravenna doves are an abstraction of the same scene: the artist strove to depict the idea of drinking doves rather than their actual appearance. Both doves are very simplified and stylized, seen strictly from the side without any clearly defined shadows. A diffused light from above illuminates the soft grey of the doves set against the deep blue of the background. The treatment of the light and abstraction of the birds and the basin make the whole scene unreal and 'dematerialized' and is eminently suited to express symbolically the concept 'Faith'. Even more striking in its photographic realism is the Pompeii mosaic (Plate 10) which is based on a famous original by a great Hellenistic painter, Sosias. The artist has clearly based his design on some very detailed studies from nature; again each individual feather is shown and one dove is still in flight just before settling on the rim of the basin. The basin itself is shown in the round and the three-dimensional effect is heightened by the shadows cast by the basin and the feet of the doves.

Unlike the Ravenna scene, this mosaic has the light source definitely on the right of the picture. The reflection of the doves in the water of the basin indicates that the artist was aiming at the maximum realistic representation of nature.

The most famous of all the Ravenna mosaics decorates the choir of the Basilica San Vitale and shows the Emperor Justinian (Plate 1) and his wife Theodora with their court. The mosaics were created at the beginning of the sixth century, that is, about a hundred years later than the mosaics in the Galla Placidia Mausoleum. They are a magnificent example of the great artistic heights reached by the early Byzantine mosaicists. The depth and perspective of the Roman mosaics have given way to concentration on the decorative richness of the scene. The two-dimensional figures in opulent draperies with glittering semi-precious stones and mother-of-pearl are set on a glowing background of gold. The stylized simplification and hieratic stiffness, emphasized by the strong contours, make this a perfect symbolic representation of the pomp of Oriental authority. The faces are still realistic in treatment but these figures are clearly not copies of paintings; the whole conception is firmly based on the decorative qualities of multicoloured and gold glass tesserae. The handling of the material shows unrivalled crafts-manship, and every mosaicist working with glass tesserae should study the technique used by these early craftsmen. Tessera is set boldly against tessera of the same colour family but in slightly differing hue, which results in an extraordinary vibrating brilliance. Contrasting colours are set in juxtaposition; tesserae are sometimes used in the pointillist manner, like dabs of pure colour: flecks of bright green or red are daringly set into areas of neutral shades. The forms and shapes are beautifully emphasized by setting the tesserae in rows which give the impression of a definite directional flow and movement; this accents the decorative pattern of shapes and colours. As we can see from some of the exciting abstract mosaics of today, mosaic material is eminently suited to this making of decorative patterns and rhythms.

In 727 the Byzantine Church issued a decree forbidding all representation of religious figures in church decoration, but mosaic as an art form survived this period of iconoclasm which lasted for about one century. Artists con-centrated on purely decorative or symbolic work, and some of the Greek craftsmen emigrated to Rome where the popes did not recognize the control exercised by the Byzantine Church. The second great Byzantine period started with the end of iconoclasm; mosaics, especially during the twelfth and thirteenth centuries, reached possibly even greater artistic heights than had those of the earlier Byzantine era. Stylistically the accent shifted towards the monumental and expressionistic, done with the great economy of means which is so characteristic of the great periods of mosaic making. In the early Byzan-tine works the religious figures were mysterious but still human, but now all remnants of classical realism disappeared and on the ceilings and apses of the churches there appeared the gigantic and awe-inspiring bearded figure of Christ as the Ruler of the World, and tremendous figures of the Virgin or the saints, sublime in their majestic tranquillity. An example of the pure Byzantine style at its greatest height is the mosaic in the apse of the Cathedral in Cefalù in Sicily (Plate 13), whose commanding presence dominates the whole church. The majestic head of Christ with the grave expressiveness of the beautiful face is a powerful symbol of a spiritual concept. The strong rhythm of the stylized lines of the cloak, and of the face and hair of Christ, emphasize the strength and power of the Pantocrator, the Ruler of the World. The luminous blue, green and black are set against the enormous expanse of gold which is so typical of the later Byzantine mosaics; a curved apse or cupola covered entirely with gold tesserae glows as if it generated its own light. The immaterial quality of this reflected light expresses superbly the other-worldliness of the Christian heaven. Roger Fry ascribes to the mosaic a unique power 'in the realization of vision. The vibrancy of effect produced by decidedly broken colour creates a definite aesthetic stimulant which, in the right surroundings, quickens religious emotion.' Whether or not the Byzantine craftsmen were conscious of the psychological power of the mosaic, there is no doubt that they had a perfect understanding of the material with which they worked and were able to give perfect expression to the intensely felt spiritualism of the Church; the mosaics which they created are without a doubt amongst the most glorious works of European art.

The association of religion and mosaic which originated in Byzantine times has been maintained to this day, although it is self-evident that such a tradition must degenerate into a sterile convention when a deeply meaningful faith no longer provides the artistic inspiration but is replaced by a mechanical copying of the style of a previous period.

A superb example of the austere yet vigorous expressionism in which Byzantine art excelled is the mosaic work in the church of the Nea Moni on Chios, dating from the eleventh century (Plate 14). Our reproduction shows the figures of Adam and Eve, a detail of 'The Descent into Limbo'. The bold stylization of the faces is immensely powerful: the strong black shadows are created solely for expressive purposes and in no way indicate from where the light is coming. They help to give the faces a severe, even grim expressiveness in accordance with the severity of the mysticism of the Eastern Church. Emphatic contours enclose areas of strong primary colour, and these contours and lines moving in strong curves give the whole composition an immensely dramatic tension (see page 65). Almost abstract shapes help to define the features (notice the curved triangle underneath the eye of Adam) and the distortions and large eyes foreshadow twentieth-century expressionism. The garments, too, are defined by almost abstract lines made up of curved rows of single tesserae. Although the tesserae used in the faces are somewhat smaller than those in the garments, compare them with the tiny stones used by the Romans in their realistic portraits (Plate 4).

Other notable mosaics in the height of the Byzantine period are preserved in Istambul (Hagia Sophia and Kahrieh Djami), in St Mark's in Venice, in Daphni near Athens, and in the Palatine Chapel in Palermo (a copy of one of the Palermo mosaics, 'Triumphal Entry of Christ in Jerusalem', can be seen in the Victoria and Albert Museum in London). One of the most moving and awe-inspiring of the late Byzantine works is the 'Virgin and Child' in the apse of the Basilica on Torcello (the island in the Venetian lagoon) which dates from the twelfth century (Plate 15). The mosaicist achieved an exceptionally dramatic effect by setting the lone slim figure of the Virgin against a vast expanse of gold. She is not surrounded by saints and angels as was the usual practice in apse decorations; the simplicity of the composition and the sombre blue of the garment set against the gold give a spectacular power to the whole mosaic. The beautifully serious face and the garment with its stylized folds show Byzantine art at its zenith. To appreciate the full power of Byzantine religious expression, compare it with the pictures of the Virgin painted by the Renaissance artists a few hundred years later.

As far as is known, the following was the technique employed by the mosaicists of the Byzantine era. First they covered the wall with a layer of plaster on which the design was scratched or painted, sometimes in full colour. This was then covered, a small area at a time, by a second layer of mortar, which consisted of a mixture of marble dust, lime and a kind of natural cement found locally. Into this the tesserae were pressed. No grout was applied to the finished mosaic. The tesserae were set at varying, carefully thought-out angles, which were determined by the source of light in the building, so that the reflected light transformed the mosaic into a living, glittering surface. In the early Byzantine period the illumination was sometimes only a dim light from an alabaster window, or candlelight, which made the interior of the church or chapel appear unreal and mysterious. The danger of the whole mosaic wall dissolving into a shimmering mess was avoided by keeping the designs severely simple, strengthened by bold contours and colour contrasts. The harsh coldness of some modern mosaics is often due to the bright and brutal lighting which takes all the life out of the mosaic material. Indirect light is best suited to a mosaic made of glass tesserae, since the shiny surface of the tesserae reflects so much more light than an ordinary painted surface.

Unfortunately many of the Byzantine mosaics have been very badly restored throughout the centuries. Damaged areas were carelessly removed and redone completely with no regard to the technique employed in the originals. The damage usually occurred when whole areas, not just individual tesserae, became detached from the wall or ceiling. Especially in the nineteenth century, such areas were not carefully repaired but simply renewed in a smooth, hard and mechanical manner. Today whole blocks are carefully removed, so that the original position of the tesserae is not disturbed, and are replaced in position after the necessary repairs have been done.

The fifteenth century saw immense political and cultural upheavals. The Moslem Turks had exerted westward pressure for over a century, and in 1453 their conquest of Constantinople brought to an end the rule of Byzantium over Eastern Christendom which had lasted for more than a thousand years. Italy became once more the religious and cultural centre of the Christian world and the beginning of the Renaissance marked the end of the Middle Ages. The intense religious mysticism of the Byzantine period, to which the mosaic had given such admirable pictorial expression, gave way to a humanistic study of man and nature. Artists began to rediscover perspective and aimed at a faithful realism or ideal representation of man based on the classical tradition of Greece and Rome, even though their subjects continued to be almost entirely religious.

For over two thousand years, from the times of classical Greece to the end of the Byzantine Empire, mosaicists had been almost exclusively Greek craftsmen who travelled all over the Mediterranean region executing mosaic commissions. Local craftsmen who had worked under the Greek experts had picked up the mosaic techniques, and with the end of the Byzantine Empire the centre of mosaic making shifted to Italy. Italian craftsmen began to open workshops of their own, notably in Venice and Rome. With the end of the artistic inspiration from the Byzantine mosaicists, Italian craftsmen concentrated mainly on copying paintings in mosaic. Renaissance artists like Giotto and Rafael all tried their hand at mosaic making, but the medium appealed to them only because of its durability. Ghirlandaio called mosaic making 'painting for eternity' and to Renaissance artists the perfect mosaic was one which was indistinguishable from a painting. But the mosaic as a creative art was dead. Practically no original works in this medium were produced after the fifteenth century, until in the twentieth century the mosaic regained its place as a creative medium in its own right. Although the Italian workshops were not artistically creative they did keep the technique alive; they became and still are today the world's centre of mosaic craftsmanship.

At various times attempts were made to revive the art of the mosaic. For instance, the activities of the Italian workshops in the seventeenth century gave Christopher Wren an idea of using mosaics for the interior of St Paul's Cathedral, but he abandoned the idea, and the present mosaics there date from the nineteenth century.

The idea of practically indestructible 'paintings' appealed to the popes of the seventeenth and eighteenth centuries. Many paintings, especially at St Peter's in Rome, were copied in mosaic, and eventually the Vatican started its own mosaic workshop. Today it is one of the biggest of the Italian workshops and has grown into a veritable mosaic factory, notable for its enormous output. Complete decorations for churches are executed there and despatched to all parts of the world. There are no less than 25,000 different shades of tesserae in its storerooms. The labelling and recording of the material alone is a major feat of organization.

The nineteenth century brought with it an enthusiasm for the middle ages and an interest in the Byzantine mosaics. Although people thought Byzantine and all pre-Gothic art rather crude, they considered the richness and durability of the glass tesserae an ideal medium in which to portray the age's achievements. Both State and Church commissioned mosaics in all the major cities of Europe; but in spite of the great volume of mosaic produced at the time, none were of great artistic value. We have seen throughout the history of mosaic how current styles of painting had influenced mosaic styles, and how the influence had not always been beneficial. The academic style of mid-nineteenth-century painting was entirely representational, neoclassical, sentimental or heroic, and mosaicists copied these paintings faithfully. The resulting works were dull both in conception and in execution. Desiccated reproductions of religious themes inspired by earlier works, or representations of historical scenes were particularly popular. Plate 16 shows a typical sentimental work of which the Victorians were so very fond. 'Finding the Saviour in the Temple', from a painting by Holman Hunt, hangs in the chapel of Clifton College in Bristol.

The Italian workshops opened branches all over Europe and the Venetian Salviati became especially active, executing work not only in Italy but also in Paris (the decorations of the Opéra), in Berlin, and in London where he was responsible for the mosaics adorning the Albert Memorial.

The nineteenth century was a busy, but on the whole sterile period of mosaic making and copying. Innumerable examples of such smooth works can be seen in most cities in which nineteenth-century buildings have been preserved. In most cases mosaics were ornaments added to the finished building instead of being conceived as part of the general architectural plan. An astonishing amount of this nineteenth-century type of kitsch is still being produced in many workshops today, particularly in Italy, aided and abetted by commissions from all over the world, especially from America. The laws of libel make it impossible for me to show reproductions of any of these works.

However, at the beginning of the twentieth century revolutionary ideas on the visual arts evolved; these ideas were to bring about a revival of the mosaic as a creative art and its liberation from the slavery to painting which had lasted for almost 500 years. Paris and Munich were particularly lively art centres, and the first decades of this century saw the birth of schools of painting whose influence is visible all around us today: the Art Nouveau movement, the Fauves, Expressionists, Cubists and Abstract painters. These movements, in spite of their often divergent aims, greatly influenced each other and the divisions between them were fluid: many leading painters went through phases in which they painted first in one and later in another style. But all the new art movements had one fundamental aim in common: they rejected the relentless realism of their predecessors.

The Art Nouveau movement, which had its origin in the late nineteenth century, was strongly decorative in character. Its influence extended to architecture and all the visual arts. One of its most original exponents was the Catalan architect Antoni Gaudí. Plate 18 shows the finial of a spire of the Cathedral of the Sagrada Familia in Barcelona, his most famous creation. It is a piece of sculpture whose undulating curves are covered with a mosaic of ceramic tiles and Venetian smalti which sparkle brilliantly in the sun. With great imaginative power he created mosaics as an integral part of his often fantastic buildings. Gaudí's work is quite unique in its baroque exuberance and inventive originality. His influence on later mosaics is most noticeable in the work of the Mexican artists which we will discuss below (page 51).

Art Nouveau was one of the sources of the Expressionist movement and distortion of natural forms was common to both schools: Art Nouveau used distortion for decorative purposes, Expressionism to produce emotional impact. The Swedish Expressionist artist Einar Forseth created the mosaic shown in Plate 17 for the Stockholm City Hall in the 1920s. Forseth uses the legendary 'Queen of Mälar' as a symbol for the city of Stockholm receiving

1 'The Emperor Justinian.' Detail from the mosaic in the choir of the Basilica San Vitale in Ravenna showing the Emperor Justinian and his wife Theodora with their court. Sixth century. A superb example of the craftsmanship of the early Byzantine mosaicists.

3 'Head of a Sea God.' A late Roman floor mosaic found in Carthage; now in the British Museum, London. *C.* A.D. 200.

◀ 2 'Huntsman.' Greek pebble floor mosaic from Pella (Macedonia). *C.* 350 B.C.

4 'Portrait of a Roman Lady.' Found in Pompeii; now in the Museo Nazionale in Naples. The mosaicist achieved an almost 'photographic' realism by the skilful use of tesserae no larger than grains of rice. The Roman mosaics show a degree of modelling and colour gradations usually reserved for painting techniques.

5 'King Darius.' Detail of the Alexander mosaic found in Pompeii, now in the Museo Nazionale in ▶ Naples. *C.* 90 B.C. The mosaic is a copy of a Greek painting of the fourth century B.C. The artist has captured the lively vigour of the battle scene by setting the tesserae in serpentine lines to accentuate movement; note especially the swish of the horses' tails.

6 'Cave Canem.' A mosaic found at Pompeii; now at the Museo Nazionale in Naples. *C.* 90 B.C.
This is a superb example of the stylized type of Roman mosaic; only three colours, red, black
and white, are used; the treatment is broad and simplified without any attempt at soft shading or
realistic modelling. The great economy of means by which the artist has brought the animal to
life shows him to have been a craftsman of the first order.

7 'Cat and Ducks.' A still life in mosaic from Pompeii; now in the Museo Nazionale in Naples. Realistic pictures of animals and scenes from mythology were the most popular subjects for mosaic decorations in the villas of the rich in Rome and Pompeii.

8 Hans Unger and Eberhard Schulze: 'St. John at the Cross.' Section of a Crucifixion (9 × 17 ft) for St Jude's Church, Wigan. 1965.

9 'Doves drinking from the Goblet of Faith.' In the Mausoleum Galla Placidia in Ravenna; fifth century A.D. The similarity of this mosaic to the one shown in Plate 11 is such that one must assume that the Byzantine artist was familiar with the Roman mosaic; note especially the position of the dove on the left of this picture. But the conception of the doves and the aims of the artists are worlds apart: the Ravenna artist depicts the idea of drinking doves rather than their actual appearance. They are simplified and stylized, seen strictly from the side, and the whole scene, unreal and 'dematerialized', is a wonderful symbol for the concept of 'Faith'.

10 'Doves round a basin.' From the house of the Faunus in Pompeii. The artist must have based his design on detailed studies from nature to achieve such a high degree of realism. The draughtsmanship is very much superior to that in the mosaic of Plate 11. The strong shadows cast on the table give the scene a three-dimensional roundness very different from the two-dimensional stylization of the Byzantine mosaic in Plate 9.

11 'Doves of Pliny.' From the Villa Hadrian, Tivoli. To accomplish a perfect realism the Roman artist has used approximately fifty times as many tesserae for the dove on the left as the Byzantine artist used for the corresponding one in Plate 9.

12 'The Good Shepherd amongst his flock.' Byzantine mosaic in the Mausoleum Galla Placidia in Ravenna; fifth century A.D. The classical calm of the composition shows the influence of Roman paintings on the early Byzantine mosaics: the idealized, beardless figure of Christ is reminiscent of Roman frescoes showing figures from classical mythology, or emperors. The feeling of Imperial nobility is emphasized by the lavish use of gold in Christ's garment and halo. It foreshadows the vast areas of gold characteristic of Byzantine mosaics at their height.

13 'Christ Pantocrator.' The mosaic covers the ceiling of the apse in the Cathedral of Cefalù in Sicily. Twelfth century. The majestic figure of Christ as the ruler of the world is a powerful symbol of the spiritual concepts of the Byzantine period at its greatest height. The luminous blue, green and black of Christ's cloak are set against the enormous expanse of gold which is typical of the later Byzantine mosaics. The gold tesserae in the curved ceiling seem to generate their own light and express perfectly the other-worldliness of the Christian heaven.

14 'Adam and Eve.' Detail from the mosaic 'Descent into Limbo' in the church of the Nea Moni, Chios. Eleventh century. Strong black contours enclose areas of red, white and blue in the garments; heavy shadows give the faces a severe expressiveness in accordance with the mysticism of the Eastern Church.

15 'Virgin and Child', in the Basilica of Torcello. Twelfth century. The artist achieved a powerful simplicity by setting the lone, slim figure of the Virgin against a plain background of pure gold. Strong stylization and the restrained sombre blues emphasize the hieratic impressiveness of the monumental figure. The perfect harmony of the religious mysticism and the artistry with which it is portrayed make this mosaic one of the glories of European art.

16 'Finding the Saviour in the Temple.' A mosaic copy of a painting by Holman Hunt. Clifton College, Bristol. Nineteenth century.

18 Antoni Gaudí: Finial of the Cathedral of the Sagrada Familia in Barcelona. Gaudí's ▶ mosaics form an integral part of his architecture; the undulating curves are characteristic of the decorative Art Nouveau movement.

17 Einar Forseth: 'The Queen of Mälar'; in the Stockholm City Hall. Although Byzantine influence is obvious, the decorative treatment of the hair and the strange large eyes are typical of the expressionism of the 1920s.

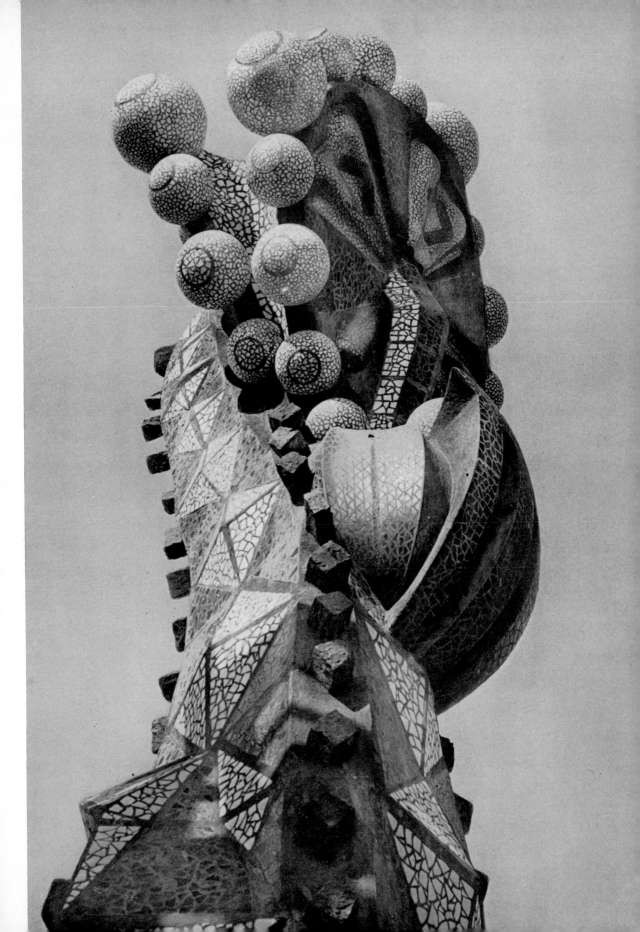

19 'The Symbol of St Luke.' Mosaic in the church of S. Apollinare in Classe, Ravenna. Seventh century. Note the astonishing similarity of Byzantine and Cubist representation of reality as illustrated on the opposite page.

20 Pablo Picasso: detail from a painting 'Nature morte a la tete de taureau rouge.' 1938.
Both Picasso and the early Ravenna artist build up the picture of the bull's head by combining in
one composition several views of it seen from different angles. The result is the idea of a bull's
head rather than its actual appearance.

21 Fernand Léger: mosaic mural on the façade of the Musée Fernand Léger, Biot, France. In its bold simplicity this is one of the most striking and impressive mosaics made in this century. The mural itself is made from smalti, the bas-relief insets with the hands and figure are made of ceramic tiles and protrude above the mosaic, casting strong shadows in the sunlight. In spite of the difference in the materials used and the varying surface levels the unity of the composition is preserved, chiefly through the strong contours which surround the simple, almost abstract shapes.

22 *Opposite, above:* Jean Bazaine: mosaic mural on the Delegations Building at Unesco House, Paris. 1958. The mosaic was set directly on the wall and the materials used are Venetian smalti and natural stones such as Mexican onyx tesserae in white and greys. The predominant colours are sky blues and mauves which form a wave-like pattern on a background of reds and yellows.

23 *Opposite:* Marc Chagall. Mosaic at the Fondation Maeght, Vence. Executed by Lino Melano. ▶

25 Joseph Young: bas-relief mosaic for the Los Angeles County Hall of Records. 1962. It represents the water sources in Los Angeles county, but the simplification of the design elements is such that the final effect is a bold abstract pattern of shapes, textures and colours. Water flows down channels in the mosaic into a pool at the base of the mural. The large dark areas are made of polished granite slabs which provide a strong contrast to the vertical brick pattern of the background. Colour is concentrated on the lower left part of the mural, an abstract composition in blue and green glass mosaic. The whole mural measures 80 ft by 20 ft.

◀ 24 Hans Unger and Eberhard Schulze: 'The Cathedral'. Mosaic panel of weathered wood and Venetian smalti on Formica.

26 Antony Hollaway: 'The Blind Beggar's Daughter of Bethnal Green'. A tile mosaic for a flat building at Bethnal Green, London. The work of Antony Hollaway is a good example of an artist executing his mosaics from small sketches which merely show the general conception of the design but leave details to the actual execution. He usually draws his design on the cement surface of the wall and then sets his tiles into the wet cement mortar. The London County Council have commissioned him to create a number of murals for their schools and housing schemes, and Mr Hollaway had to co-operate closely with the architects to fulfil their explicit requirements, often within a very tight budget.

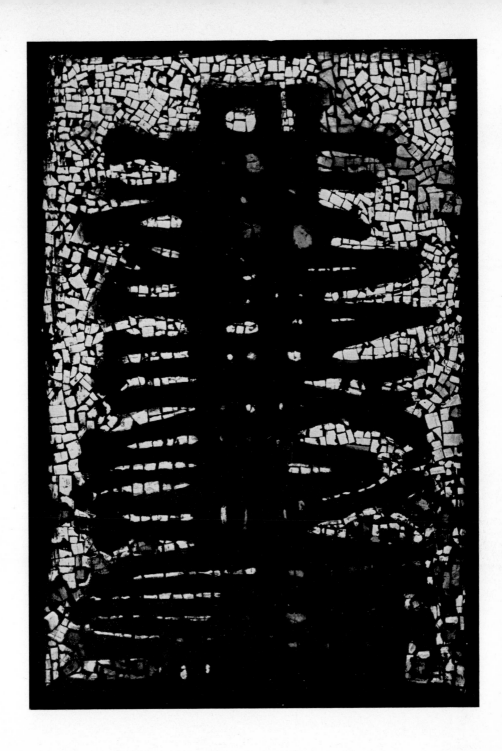

27 Antony Hollaway: 'Winter'. A translucent glass mosaic which he created for the British Artist Craftsmen Exhibition sponsored by the Smithsonian Institution. Cut pieces of stained glass have been glued with epoxy resin to a $\frac{1}{4}$-inch plate glass sheet.

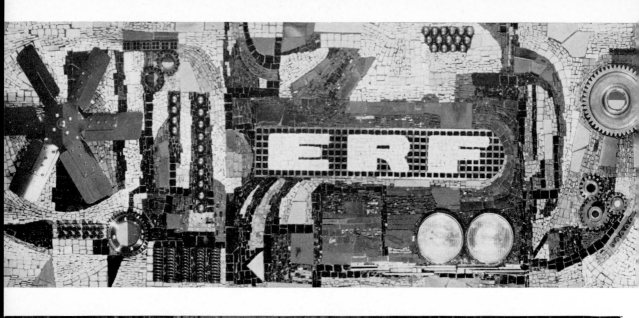

29 A mural at the Olivetti factory, Milan, designed by Giovanni Pintori, executed by Giulio Padoan. The simple typographical design is very much in keeping with the style of Olivetti's printed publicity.

◄ 28 Hans Unger & Eberhard Schulze: mosaic panel for E.R.F., manufacturers of commercial motor vehicles. Actual engine parts are incorporated in the panel. Design consultants: Stevenson-Ward.

◄ 28a Hans Unger & Eberhard Schulze: mosaic commissioned by Bison Concrete Ltd. for use as a calendar.

30 Robert Stewart: mosaic decoration for the swimming pool on the P. & O. Orient Line S.S. *Oriana*, commissioned by the Design Research Unit, who were responsible for the interior design of the liner. Mr Stewart's bold design of abstract shapes is reminiscent of oriental calligraphy. Close co-operation between mosaicist and architects resulted in a successful integration of the mosaic work into the general design of the ship.

31 Juan O'Gorman: Library of University City, Mexico D.F. 1952. The problems connected with the correct scale of the individual design elements in a mosaic measuring 140 ft by 90 ft were immense: e.g. O'Gorman had to design all his figures proportionally wider than their height in order to correct optical illusion when they were viewed from the ground. The mosaic was made in the reverse method: O'Gorman drew the full-scale design on paper which was then cut into pieces one metre square, a wooden form was built around each section of paper and the mosaic laid to cover the whole section; when this was completed concrete was poured on to it. The finished panels were hung on steel hooks protruding from the wall of the building; the wall was covered with a layer of cement and the panels pressed into it. The mosaic material is mainly local rock, lava, obsidian, marble and blue glass, each tessera measuring about 2 sq. in.

32 Juan O'Gorman: stone mosaic covering the walls of his own house in Mexico. Motifs taken from Mexican folk art and ancient Aztec symbols have been used with mastery to create a wholly original work. O'Gorman is as successful as Gaudí was in achieving a complete integration of architecture and mosaic bas-reliefs.

33 Hans Unger and Eberhard Schulze: mosaic mural for the canteen of Penguin Books Ltd, Harmondsworth, Middlesex. 1964. The orange, green and turquoise represent the colours of the
Penguin paperbacks. Venetian smalti are used, together with ceramic tiles on which stained glass
has been fused, as described in Chapter 2. To intensify their impact the colour areas are set

against black-and-white shapes and a neutral grey background of pieces of slate and a collage of highly polished typefaces, printing blocks and linotype pages used for printing the Penguin paperbacks. Individual tesserae and complete areas are protruding to give a bas-relief effect to the whole mural.

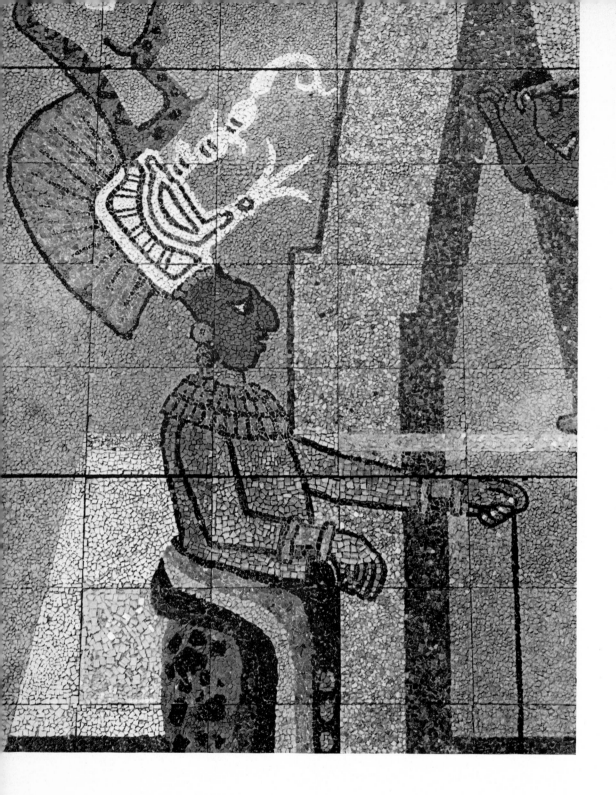

34 José Chávez Morado: detail of a mural, 'The World of the Maya', on the building of the Secretariat of Communications and Public Works, Mexico D.F. 1953. The mural consists of concrete slabs into which pieces of natural stone, glazed ceramic tiles and glass have been embedded.

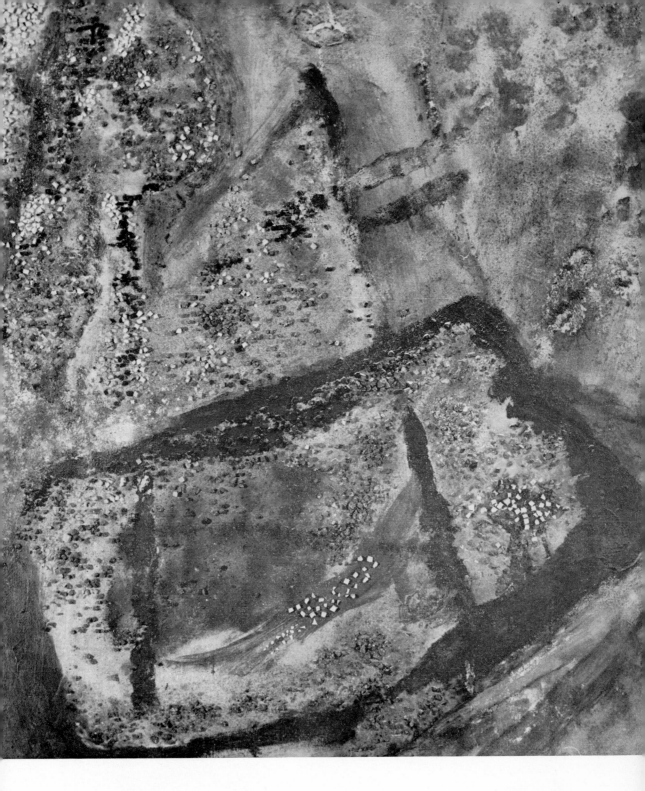

35 Jeanne Reynal: 'Morning in Mexico'. 1952. Under the influence of the action painters, Jeanne Reynal uses mosaic tesserae very much as the 'dribblers' use paint. She spreads a coat of tinted mortar on a wooden or masonite base and, taking a handful of tesserae, dribbles them on to the wet mortar. When the mortar is just beginning to set she taps the tesserae into the 'bed' and adds individual tesserae to intensify the colour in specific areas.

36 Boys of the University College School, London, at work on a paper mosaic mural.

37 The cartoon from which the mural illustrated in Plate 33 was made. The cartoon measures 18 in. by 12 in.

tribute from East and West. The rich blue of the garment of the colossal figure is set against a vast expanse of gold which covers almost the whole of the wall space. This clearly shows the influence of Byzantine mosaics, particularly the Virgin in the Cathedral of Torcello (Plate 15). But the distortion of the figure, the decorative treatment of the hair, the strange large eyes belong to the Expressionism of that period. In spite of the Byzantine influence the mosaic is twentieth-century in feeling, and Forseth has used the mosaic medium well for the stylized, monumental treatment of the human figure. A more recent work by Forseth is the marble mosaic floor in the Chapel of Unity in Coventry Cathedral.

Artists of the Art Nouveau movement had been greatly influenced by the decorative stylization and bold simplification of the Japanese woodcuts. Similarly the Fauves and Expressionists were attracted to medieval art, especially to the woodcuts and stained glass windows. The painter Rouault actually started his career as a stained glass artist. As a result of these influences modern paintings showed a broad and simplified treatment of masses and a new approach to colour. Medieval artists had often used colour for its emotional power and symbolic significance rather than to depict objects realistically. Already at the end of the nineteenth century the French painter Seurat had drawn attention to the superb colour technique of the Byzantine mosaicists. As we have seen, the Byzantines arranged their compositions so as to form strong patterns of colours and shapes. Now, in the twentieth century, painters again explored the emotional and decorative effect of colour. It was made to transcend the object depicted and was given a life of its own, capable of expressing the mysterious world of the spirit and personal feelings. Finally the complete break with tradition was made when colour, shapes and lines no longer portrayed recognizable objects but were used solely to express emotional and spiritual experience or to create decorative patterns: abstract art was born.

The different styles of abstract painting spread throughout Europe and America during the years before the Second World War. After the war Paris became the centre of an even greater output of important abstract works. The general acceptance of abstract art by the public is probably the most important single cause of the revitalization of the mosaic in this century. It is the ideal medium in which to create powerful effects by the use of strong colour areas and well-defined abstract shapes.

The artistic situation at the end of the nineteenth century has certain similarities to that at the end of the Roman Empire: the reaction of the Byzantine and the Cubist artists against the realism of the preceding age also ran on parallel lines. An astonishing example illustrating this similarity is shown in Plates 19 and 20. The mosaic 'The Symbol of St Luke' in the Ravenna church of San Apollinare in Classe dates from the seventh century A.D.; the 'Head of a Bull' is a detail from a picture which Picasso painted in 1938. The Ravenna mosaicist rejected naturalistic perspective in favour of a conceptual notion of reality by combining different views of the bull's head in one composition: the head and eye are shown in profile whereas the horns, nostrils and mouth are seen full-face. Exactly in the same manner Picasso represented three-dimensional reality by assembling several two-dimensional views of the same object seen from different angles. In both cases the result is the idea of a bull's head rather than its actual appearance.

The prismatic, fragmented representation of reality by the Cubists has a certain affinity in feeling with a mosaic composed of glass cubes. There is a strongly decorative side to the work of the Cubist painters and sculptors which affected the mosaic as well as many other forms of modern design; their collages and experiments with textures, their relief constructions and novel use of glass, wood and metal started a new awareness of surface textures and the tactile quality of different types of material (Plates 24 and 33).

At the beginning of his career, the Cubist painter Fernand Léger was under the influence of the Fauves and as a result colour played an important part in his work throughout his life. He became greatly interested in the marriage of architecture and painting; he once called painting a 'conception of coloured planes', a view clearly in sympathy with modern architecture. A blank wall was 'a dead, anonymous surface' to him and he defined in detail his ideas on colour in architecture as a space-creating element which overcomes the rigidity of a building: green, light blue and grey increase the feeling of space; orange, red and purple lessen it. A black wall comes forward, a white one recedes. Pale shades create a feeling of distance, strong, pure colours a feeling of nearness. Texture, too, has its effect on the feeling of space: because the grained texture of a surface is visible from the distance it appears closer than a smooth surface. Large murals, like the one illustrated in Plate 21, gave Léger the opportunity to create very powerful decorative designs in which he could set strong shapes and areas of pure colour against each other. The illustration shows the façade of the Musée Fernand Léger in Biot, France. His abstractions are usually based on some definite motifs: here we can recognize a landscape with trees, houses, roads and a lake. However, the natural forms are simplified and abstracted to such a degree that clearly his interest lay foremost in the relationship of shapes and colours to each other. The powerful simplicity of Léger's creations and their intelligent integration into the whole architectural concept of a building make his mosaic work the most outstanding of this century.

Another eminent abstract artist who has created mosaics is the French painter Jean Bazaine. In 1958 he was commissioned to design a mosaic mural for the Unesco building in Paris (Plate 22). Bazaine, a pupil of Bonnard, was brought up in the tradition of the French Impressionists and he shares their preoccupation with light and colour. In the Unesco mosaic he aimed at a design whose rhythmical pattern of colours and abstract shapes was in harmony with the long horizontal wall space and with the Japanese garden which it faces. Bazaine's mosaic still has a strongly painterly quality about it; the subtle shadings and dynamic brush strokes of his cartoon are clearly discernible in the mural. Although Bazaine actively collaborated with the mosaicist who executed the work, a slight feeling remains that the mural is a painting translated into a mosaic rather than a mosaic conceived as such; one misses the feeling of inevitability imposed by the medium itself. The fundamental importance of the union of the art and craft sides of mosaic making, of the interdependence of design and material will be more fully discussed in Chapter 4. However, with these reservations, Bazaine's Unesco mosaic is an impressive work.

An attempt to create a mosaic in which design and mosaic material are mutually dependent is shown in Plate 33. It is a mural which the author and Eberhard Schulze designed and executed for the canteen of Penguin Books at Harmondsworth near London. The purely abstract composition consists of large areas of bright orange, green and turquoise, representing the colours of the Penguin paperbacks. To intensify the colour impact these areas are set against contrasting shapes in black and white and surrounded by a background of different shades of grey. Emphasis on the tactile appeal of the mosaic medium is achieved by the use of collage: printing blocks, type faces and complete Linotype pages are used extensively together with the traditional mosaic materials of glass smalti, ceramic tiles and slate. Individual tesserae, blocks and whole areas project from the foundation to create a bas-relief effect and to give the whole mural a sculptural feeling. The aim was to integrate collage and mosaic into a unified composition with equal stress on the power of the design and the attraction of the material.

Mexico is one of the few countries which, in modern times, has evolved a national style of mosaic. The excellent work done in that country has been but little influenced by the modern schools of painting in Europe and North America. One of the most prominent Mexican mosaicists is Juan O'Gorman. Like Gaudí at the beginning of this century, O'Gorman treats the mosaic very much as an architectural theme: a wall is a surface to be embellished and colour is an integral part of architecture. Mexico has a strong tradition of exuberant decoration which began with the sculptured walls of the Maya temples and Aztec symbolic carvings; it was further developed during the baroque period after the Spanish conquest, and this tradition is still kept alive in the vivacious folk art of Mexico. Mural painting was given a great impetus when Diego Rivera and Clemente Orozco were commissioned in the 1920s to paint large frescoes on several public buildings. Plate 31 shows the Library of University City in Mexico D.F. covered entirely by the mosaics of Juan O'Gorman. It was completed in 1952. This work clearly illustrates O'Gorman's opposition to a puritan functionalism in architecture and his unashamed love of decoration, giving pleasure by rich form and colour. The theme of this mosaic is the history of ideas in Mexico.

In the 1940s new trends in painting appeared in the United States. Political events in Europe and the outbreak of the Second World War forced many leading European artists to seek refuge in America. Their own work and their influence on the work of American artists led to the school of action painting; the vitality of the painting process itself was its main preoccupation. At a first glance it seems unlikely that the unconscious, automatic painting method of the action painters could influence the deliberate and often laborious process of mosaic making. However, the American mosaicist Jeanne Reynal who had had close personal ties with the New York action painters started to use mosaic tesserae very much as the 'dribblers' used paint: Plate 35 shows one of her mosaic panels, 'Morning in Mexico', which she did in 1952. A sharp-edged solid material like a cube of glass is not really a suitable medium for 'action' work with its accent on free movement; but Jeanne Reynal cuts most of her smalti tesserae to a tiny size so that they lose their definite rectangular shape and become glittering dots of colour, which she sets into a background of brightly coloured cement or plastic. It is her aim to free the mosaic entirely from its dependence on the painted cartoon and compose mosaics in which she can capture 'the poetry of light'. Miss Reynal deserves respect since her work and thoughts on light and texture are based on a thorough knowledge and practical experience of the various mosaic techniques. But in my view the fortuitous application of tesserae is liable to become a merely superficial decoration of the wall surface. Action painting has brought a new freedom and vigour to modern art; but it rejects completely planned design and composition. It is doubtful whether this school of painting will have much influence on a medium whose particular qualities demand the discipline of a firm design.

In the last few pages I have tried to show how modern art movements have changed the appearance of the mosaic. Equally influential were the changes in architectural thinking. The nineteenth century had been unduly preoccupied with the appearance of a building; form in architecture was quite unrelated to function and buildings were covered with decorations and ornaments which were usually copied from previous ages.

In healthy opposition against the sham façade of the nineteenth century, the pioneers of the new architecture demanded that function determined the form of a building. The wide use of steel, glass and reinforced concrete revolutionized construction methods and the great exponents of functional architecture created inspired structures of unadorned simplicity. But the purity of functionalism was lost when some architects, without properly understanding its aims, used its outer manifestations as a short cut to a so-called modernism. The result was the arid style of rectangular dreariness which disfigures so many of our cities today.

Lack of humanity in buildings which have been treated solely as problems of function and construction is inevitable. The slender elegance of mechanical precision may be a perfect expression of the age of science, mass production and technology: but the important emotional side of man is unsatisfied, the side which responds to and is stimulated by art. Architects like Le Corbusier and Gropius called for a closer co-operation between art and architecture, and groups of artists and architects founded societies to promote their synthesis. But on the whole, this separation continues: the artist works in the isolation of his studio and occasionally a work of art is introduced into a building as an afterthought.

In all great architecture the aesthetic and the functional are blended into one. It is in this context that the mosaic has its legitimate place as an integral part of architecture. To achieve this integration fully the mosaicist must be fully aware of his position: he has to create his work within the framework of the architect's conception of the building, otherwise the mosaic, however admirable in itself, might undermine the architect's intentions. Only the architect knows the aesthetic and functional needs of his building: the correct spatial relationships and use of colour, the placing of an accent or focal point. The close co-operation of architect and artist in the initial stages will prevent the mosaic from becoming an addition to the building instead of being an inseparable part of it.

The future development of our cities will separate the fast moving traffic from the pedestrian. Buildings on two entirely different scales, at present intermingled, will form distinct units; the superhuman scale of the airport, the gigantic bridges, the towering office block will contrast with the human scale of the shopping centres, the piazzas and streets where people walk and can enjoy leisure. The mosaic will have its own place in this new setting. Its special qualities of boldness combined with beauty of texture and interesting detail of design will give the citizen a new delight as part of his daily existence.

2 Materials

Manufactured Materials

SMALTI The coloured glass tessera has lost none of its appeal since the fourth century A.D. when it took the place of marble and stone as the most widely used mosaic material. It is clean, is almost indestructible both in and out of doors and has qualities of colour, texture and reflective ability that are unequalled by any other material. Its appeal to the sense of touch is immediate: the first thing any visitor to a mosaic workshop will do is to handle the glass cubes with delight.

The most beautiful and expensive of the glass tesserae are the Venetian or Byzantine *smalti* (which is Italian for enamels). They are manufactured almost exclusively in Italy. The centre of the glass-making industry is Venice and the island of Murano across the Venetian lagoon. The exact details of the manufacturing process are secrets handed down from generation to generation, but here is a general outline of the operation. The basic material of all glass is silica, to which alkaline substances such as potash-lead or soda-lime are added. The addition of oxide of tin makes the glass opaque. Meta oxides are the only colouring agents; dyes are never used. These make the tesserae entirely light-proof. Here are a few examples of metal oxides and their corresponding colours:

Blue: cobalt oxide

Blue-Green: cobalt oxide with added cupric oxide

Ruby: selenium dioxide, cadmium sulphide, gold chloride

Purple: manganese dioxide, tellurium oxide

Pink: selenium oxide

Yellow: iron oxide, antimoniate of lead, cerium dioxide, titanium dioxide, uranium oxide

Green: copper oxide, copper carbonate, chromium oxide.

The silica with the alkaline and metal oxide additions is melted down in a furnace at very carefully controlled temperatures which vary according to the intended colour. When the melting process has been completed the viscous glass mixture is poured into a flat metal dish for cooling; this, too, has to take place at a very carefully controlled rate. The resulting glass disc resembles a thick pancake in size and shape. Girls working mechanical choppers cut these discs into cubes measuring about $\frac{1}{2} \times \frac{1}{4} \times \frac{1}{4}$ in. Two sides of each cube (the top and bottom of the original 'pancake') are fairly smooth; the other sides, which are the fractured edges, are uneven. It is these fractured surfaces which reveal the brilliant colour of the glass and are usually exposed in setting the mosaic. They give the smalti reflective quality, depth of colour and sparkle superior to those of any other substance. Modern smalti have a greater colour intensity and range than those made in Byzantine times. Incidentally, manufacturers who supply workshops specializing in restoration work are able to reproduce the exact colours and textures of the ancient Byzantine glass by adding sand and other substances to the glass mixture.

The colour range of the smalti is very extensive; most manufacturers have as many as 5,000 colours in stock and the Vatican workshops have a store of 25,000 different shades. With such an enormous colour range the most subtle colour gradations can be achieved. The professional mosaicist is likely to need a minimum of 200 to 300 shades. The most brilliant smalti are the oranges, yellows and blues, but all the colours of the rainbow are available, with the exception of brilliant violet: no oxide has been discovered capable of producing a violet comparable in intensity with the other shades.

Gold smalti are made by a different process: unlike the pigment in ordinary smalti the gold does not go through the whole cube but consists of gold leaf between two layers of glass. This is the manufacturing process: first, the glass blower blows a very thin sphere of clear glass. After cooling, this is cut by hand into smaller pieces on which the gold leaf is placed and heated for better adhesion to the glass. Then a thick layer of molten glass is poured on top of the gold leaf and pressed so that the gold leaf is sandwiched between the two layers of glass; this will protect it from damage and atmospheric influences. More than two dozen shades of gold are available, ranging from light yellowish to rich coppery hues. The surface varies from smooth to several types of uneven textures such as 'granulated' and 'ancient'. Tesserae made from other metals such as silver, aluminium and copper are produced by a similar process. Further diversity is obtained by varying the backing glass from colourless to shades of bright green and turquoise; red backing, too, has been used for many centuries to enhance the richness of the gold tesserae.

Normally a metal tessera is set with its thin layer of glass uppermost, but for special effects the cube can be reversed; the light will then be reflected by the metal through the thick layer of glass and will give the tessera a jewel-like sparkle. This effect must be used with great restraint to avoid gaudiness.

Smalti are sold by weight and about three pounds will cover one square foot. Various colours are grouped together according to their price as follows:

Gold
Silver
Imperial Colours (reds, oranges and yellows)
Flesh Colours (light and dark flesh tints)
Fine Colours (pure white, greens and blues)
Ordinary Colours (blacks, greys, browns, dark yellows, greens, blues and off-whites)

The gold smalti are the most expensive tesserae and the 'ordinary' colours the cheapest.

VITREOUS GLASS MOSAIC These machine-made glass tesserae are thinner and considerably cheaper than smalti. They are manufactured in many countries besides Italy. Molten glass with its alkaline and metal oxide additions is poured into waffle-like forms and pressed; the resulting tesserae are approximately $\frac{3}{4}$ in. square and $\frac{1}{8}$ in. thick (some manufacturers also make them in smaller or larger sizes). The pressed upper side is smooth, the underside is bevelled and grooved which allows the adhesive to get a better grip. These vitreous glass tesserae are today widely used for wall cladding and are ideal for all functional mosaics (such as tabletops) on which a smooth surface is desired. Although the oranges and yellows are very brilliant the vitreous tesserae are inferior to the smalti tesserae in colour intensity and, more important, in reflective quality, since the surface of each cube is quite flat. They contain a greater proportion of sand and some of them appear rather grainy, but they are a useful and popular mosaic material, sold at a reasonable price. They are available in about fifty shades and a pound and a half to two pounds will cover one square foot. They are usually sold by the square foot since they are widely used by the building trade. For this reason they are also sold mounted on sheets of paper so that a whole sheet with the mosaic can be embedded into the mortar on a flat wall or around a pillar. The method used is similar to that described on page 83 under the heading 'Reverse Method'.

CERAMIC TILES   Tiles are a very inexpensive mosaic material and ordinary household tiles can be used to great effect. For economic reasons, most large murals are made from ceramic tiles, perhaps enlivened by smaller areas of vitreous glass or smalti in those parts of the mosaic where a brilliantly coloured detail needs emphasis.

Ceramic tiles are usually 4-in. or 6-in. squares of fired clay, covered with a matt or glossy glaze finish; only the surface is coloured. The standard commercial ceramic tile is usually adequate for outdoor use, although special frost-proof tiles are made by some tile manufacturers. The colour range of commercial ceramic tiles is limited and the brilliant colours of the glass tesserae are not normally available. Apart from the fact that the tiles themselves are so much cheaper than glass tesserae, a further economic advantage is their greater size which enables one to cover a much larger area in a given time.

Even after they have been cut or broken up, commercial tiles still retain their machine-finished look. This quality can be used effectively to set off materials of a livelier texture and surface. However, if one finds this machine finish disturbing and wants to use tiles of more exciting colour and texture, one can obtain hand-made tiles from special ceramic tile shops which sell a variety of hand-made tiles or will make them to one's own specifications.

If you want to be entirely independent of available supplies it is possible to make your own ceramic mosaic material. After the initial outlay for a kiln it is a very inexpensive way of producing tesserae and tiles and, after the necessary experience has been acquired, you will be able to produce the colours and textures desired instead of making do with what is commercially available. The details of the various glazing and firing techniques are beyond the scope of this book and a specialized book on ceramics such as Kenneth Clark's *Practical Pottery and Ceramics* should be consulted.

I should, however, like to give a short description of a majolica technique which is somewhat different from the standard methods used for producing ceramic glazes. Although it is not a cheap process it is quickly mastered and the results are strikingly beautiful. It consists of placing smalti or pieces of cut stained glass (known as 'Antique' glass in the trade) on a white commercial tile and melting it in the kiln at a temperature of approximately 1050° C. (1922° F.), varying according to the type of glass used. By putting the pieces of stained glass on the tile one can immediately see the colour effect; this is not possible if glazing powders are used, since their colour is brought out only during the firing. The white surface of the tile reflects the maximum amount of light so that the stained glass loses little of its depth and brilliance of colour; tiles produced in this manner can be as rich in colour as smalti. An infinite variety of extremely beautiful colour combinations can be obtained by mixing variously coloured pieces of stained glass: by placing them next to each other or by overlapping them, by pounding them in a mortar or by placing a few pieces of actual smalti on pieces of stained glass. By varying the thickness of the stained glass pieces the machine-finished surface of the commercial tile can be completely obliterated and any number of different and exciting textures can be obtained. Since you can match the exact shades of the smalti, tiles produced in this manner are ideal for use in conjunction with smalti when you wish to have variety in the size of the mosaic material.

Tiles made in this manner usually show a 'crazing' effect of fine or deeper cracks which adds an interesting texture to the surface. Do not put too much glass or smalti on to each tile, since the melting glass might run across and over the tile edge on to the kiln shelf. Always paint the shelves with a coat of water and powdered flint to make it easier to remove any glass which might have run on to the shelf.

FLOOR TILES   These tiles are thicker than the ceramic tiles described in the previous section. The colour goes through the whole tile, since the pigment is mixed with the clay from which the tiles are made. They are not glazed. Within the limit of their small colour range and matt finish they are a useful material, especially for large murals. But a word of warning: as a rule these 'encaustic' tiles are not impervious to water and are therefore not frost-proof.

SMALL CERAMIC TESSERAE   Many tile merchants also stock ceramic mosaic tesserae, similar in size to the vitreous glass tesserae, i.e. roughly $\frac{3}{4}$ in. square. Two different types are made: the vitrified unglazed ceramic mosaic and glazed ceramic tesserae which look like miniature tiles. They are usually limited to pastel shades and black and white and do not include any of the brilliant glass tesserae colours.

A useful material if used with discretion is stained glass backed with metal leaf: the metal acts as a light reflector and brings out the brilliance of the glass. Translucent plastics, such as Perspex, which are available in many bright shades can also be used, provided they are fixed on a light-coloured base.

Natural Materials

PEBBLES   As mentioned in the chapter on the history of the mosaic, natural pebbles, rounded by sea or river water, were used for making floor mosaics some four or five thousand years ago and still make an attractive material for floor mosaics or sophisticated panels. Pebbles can be found on beaches or in river beds, but it is essential to grade them according to shade and size before using them.

MARBLE   Marble has also been used for thousands of years as a decorative material of great beauty and durability. The grain and pattern of marble are best seen when the surface has been highly polished. Since cutting marble is not an easy process, it is advisable to buy scraps of polished marble from marble masons. Rich dark greens and browns are particularly attractive and many shades of grey, ranging from near-white to near-black, can be found.

   Many builders' merchants stock small ready-cut marble bricks known as 'rustic marble'. They are imported from Italy and measure about $4\frac{1}{2} \times 1 \times \frac{1}{2}$ in. Their colours range from white to various shades of grey and ochre and they have an attractive grainy or crystalline surface texture.

MARBLE TESSERAE   Small marble cubes of a similar size to smalti are available in a number of pastel colours: greys, whites, pinks, light browns, grey-greens. Their surface is often quite rough, which gives a whole area covered in marble tesserae an exciting surface texture. If you want to intensify their colour you can varnish the completed mosaic with a colourless varnish.

SLATE   Slate in subtle greys from reddish or bluish to green hues can be obtained from most builders' merchants or special slate suppliers. Slate is usually thinner than marble and can be cut much more easily. It is very effective for covering a large area and the natural matt surface makes a good contrast to the high gloss of tiles or glass tesserae. An unsuspected sombre richness can be achieved by painting slate with a non-yellowing cellulose varnish or synthetic resin such as polyester. A very lively and strongly directional pattern can be created by cutting thin strips of slate and setting them close together with their thin edges uppermost.

   Natural stones and minerals such as granite, quartz, obsidian, lava and asbestos, all types of natural, weathered or polished wood, mother-of-pearl and many types of shells can all be used in mosaic making.

3 Tools and methods of cutting the material

The necessary relationship of the size of the tesserae or pieces of stone, etc., to the final size of the completed mosaic is obvious: on a large mural which will be viewed from a fair distance and where a simple monumental effect is desired, uncut glass tesserae and large pieces of tile, stone, marble or slate can be used. On the other hand, a small mosaic panel made entirely from uncut material will look crude. If the mosaic is to be viewed from close to, or if the design requires detailed work, the material will have to be shaped by cutting.

The principle of cutting a hard material like glass or stone is this: pressure is set up by two opposing forces such as the jaws of a pair of pincers or a hammer striking the material as it rests on a sharp-edged anvil (known as a hardie). Along a line between the two points of pressure the molecular structure of the material is weakened and a split results.

FIG I Mosaic hammer (A); hardie, front view (B); side view (C) The tungsten-carbide tips are shown in black

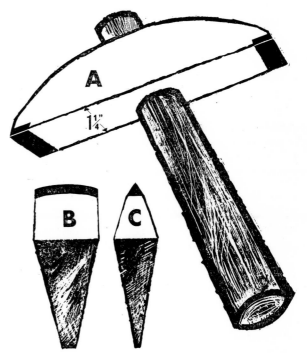

Smalti and vitreous glass tesserae

The most accurate tools for cutting glass tesserae are a type of stone mason's hammer and a hardie (Fig. 1). The hammer is slightly curved and has two sharpened tips made from tungsten-carbide alloy, so that it is not easily blunted. It should weigh about 4 pounds. A hardie is similar to an inverted chisel, with a slightly curved cutting edge which is made from tungsten-

FIG 2
Hardie set into a wooden log about 3½ ft high

carbide. It should be set into a heavy wooden log about 3½ ft high (see Fig 2); this is a comfortable height for working in a standing position and enables the forearm to work loosely, without strain. These tools can be imported through Italian smalti suppliers, or you can get them made to your own specifications by a firm of tungsten-carbide tool makers. To cut glass tesserae accurately takes practice, and the beginner should not be discouraged if the glass shatters completely under the first blow of the hammer. A few tips will help: place the tessera on the hardie, holding it firmly between thumb and forefinger; it should be held level at an angle of 90 degrees to the cutting edge of the hardie. Aim a light blow of the hammer on a point of the tessera exactly above the cutting edge of the hardie.

FIG 3
Spring-type, toggle-jointed mosaic clippers

Although for the most accurate work hammer and hardie should be used, a specially designed pair of adjustable clippers is available from special mosaic shops or tile merchants (Fig. 3). These spring-type, toggle-jointed cutters are made from specially hardened steel. By means of setting screws the width between the cutting edges can be adjusted to the thickness of the material which you want to cut. When using these clippers, do not put the cutting edges right across the whole width of the tessera, but as near to its edge as possible and in line with the direction in which you want the glass to split. Tesserae can be cut with these clippers accurately enough for most requirements and it is certainly the quickest and most convenient method. A simpler type of mosaic cutters resembles an ordinary pair of pincers but is also made of a specially hardened metal. It is not spring-operated and is therefore likely to tire your hands sooner than the spring-type clippers. A new Japanese 7½ in. type of nippers (Fig. 4) with carbide tips has just come on the market and can be highly recommended. Ordinary household pincers are not very suitable since glass, one of the hardest materials known, will blunt them within a very short time.

FIG 4
Spring-type Japanese nippers

TILES   The tools needed for tile cutting are tile cutters or glass cutters and a pair of pincers. These tools are available in all tool shops. Tile cutters

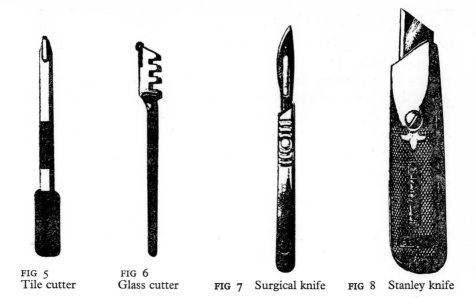

FIG 5
Tile cutter

FIG 6
Glass cutter

FIG 7 Surgical knife

FIG 8 Stanley knife

(Fig. 5) consist of a square pencil-like stem with a tungsten-carbide tip with which to score the glazed surface of the tile. A glass cutter (Fig. 6) has a little tungsten-carbide wheel at the top and can also be used for tile cutting. To score a line apply only light pressure and work in one rapid movement: the scoring will alter the molecular structure of the glazed surface but is not meant actually to cut the tile (Fig. 9).

For larger pieces run the tile cutter along a metal rule or straight edge. To break the tile, put it on a straight piece of wood or along the edge of a working table with the scored line exactly above the edge of the wood and apply pressure with the hands on either side of the scored line (Fig. 10). For breaking off smaller strips of tile use a pair of pincers or nippers. Put the cutting edges of the nippers on the scored line near the edge of the tile and apply firm pressure; the tile will break along the line. Ordinary household pincers can be used for nipping off bits of tile if the break is not clean, but again, they will get blunt rapidly if used frequently.

FIG 9 Scoring the tile with a glass cutter

FIG 10 Breaking the scored tile

MARBLE AND STONE, ETC. These materials will not split as neatly and accurately as glass and tiles. Marble masons use power tools such as saws and grinders which are not a practical proposition for the ordinary mosaicist. For cutting small pieces use the hammer and hardie as described in the section on glass tesserae cutting. Before splitting larger pieces, score a line on both sides of the material with a small chisel and hammer. Rest the piece which you want to split on two pieces of wood so that the scored line does not lie on the supporting table and then split the marble or stone by careful hammer blows along the scored line.

PLASTIC The technique for scoring and cutting Perspex and other hard plastic materials is similar to that used for cutting glass tesserae. Perspex can also be sawn with a hack saw, pad saw or, if a powered saw is available, use the 'combination' blade (at the lowest revs. since too much friction will melt the Perspex). Thin machine oil makes a good lubricant and coolant when cutting Perspex.

4 Designing the cartoon

In the chapter on the history of mosaic I have tried to show the interdependence of mosaic and mosaic material. Painting, as the more widespread form of artistic expression, has had an influence on the mosaic throughout the ages, though this influence was fairly limited during the Byzantine era. During that period the mosaicist was both artist and craftsman and the conception of each mosaic was based firmly on the special character of the material used. An equally important reason for the outstanding height of perfection reached by the Byzantine mosaics was the fact that they were created as an integral part of the architecture in which they were set.

A mosaic up to a certain size can be considered as a self-contained 'picture' in the same way as one would consider an oil painting which has been painted without reference to the particular surrounding space where it is going to be hung. But as soon as the mosaic becomes a mural it must be subordinate to the general plan of the building and its architectural conception. If it is to be more than an afterthought for covering an empty space, very close co-operation between architect and artist right from the beginning is absolutely essential: before he even thinks of the mosaic design the artist must make himself familiar with the architect's intention as to the function of the mosaic in the general plan of the building. He must study carefully the conditions of space and light and the colours and textures of the materials to be used in the space surrounding the mosaic.

We have also seen how rapidly mosaic as a creative art declined every time the special character of the material was ignored and the mosaicist tried to imitate in glass or stone the softer and more flexible technique of painting. When designing the cartoon (i.e. the preparatory painting to be used as the basis for making the mosaic) it is essential to look closely at both the positive qualities and the limitations of the material itself. The power and quality of the material must not be allowed to compete for attention with the design itself but both must be used creatively so as to bring them into active relation with each other. This creative relationship between design, material and the actual craft of setting the material is the most important problem that every mosaicist has to tackle.

When starting your design you must never forget that the cartoon is only a preparatory sketch on which the final mosaic will be based: it is not a finished painting in its own right. Making mosaics is a craft and a great deal of the creative process takes place during the actual setting of the tesserae or other materials. This means that too accurate a cartoon is likely to be a hindrance rather than a help in achieving a lively and vigorous mosaic. The copying of a detailed painting in which practically each stone has been painted will result in a deadly flat and mechanical mosaic. Spontaneity is a considerable factor in creating an exciting and lively work.

Let us first consider glass tesserae. Their size today is much the same as it has been for more than 2,000 years and for a good reason: a tessera $\frac{1}{2}$ in. to $\frac{3}{4}$ in. square is large enough for the colour area to have an impact which will not be neutralized by the crevices between the tesserae; on the other hand it is small enough to enable the mosaicist to give his work a suitable degree of fine detail. When designing the cartoon for mosaic it is important always to keep in mind that a cube of glass or stone is a hard, strong material with well-defined sharp edges. Correspondingly, the design should be simple, strong and bold and any attempt at soft naturalistic rendering of subjects should be avoided. A stylized, monumental approach with emphasis on pattern rather than chiaroscuro and soft shading is best suited to the material.

Mosaic work has a certain affinity to stained glass windows: areas of glowing colours can be set against each other to great effect, can merge into each other, can be separated and strengthened by bold contours or set against a black, white or neutral shade to strengthen the colour impact by contrast. Mosaic is more suitable than almost any other material for covering large areas of one colour; by choosing tesserae of the same colour but slightly differing hue a colour vibration is set up which gives glass mosaic its characteristic sparkle and life. Texture will also help to enliven a large area. It can be emphasized or played down but because of the nature of glass tesserae it can never be eliminated and should therefore be used creatively. The natural texture of the tesserae can be further varied by setting some of them or whole areas at different heights or by standing some tesserae on end, thereby creating a three-dimensional effect similar to a bas-relief (see Plates 21, 25, 32 and 33). The shadows cast by the raised tesserae will create this sculptural effect; it is therefore essential to consider carefully the source of light so as to be able to gauge the strength and length of the shadows.

The source of light plays an equally important part when planning light reflection of the tesserae. By varying the angles at which you set the tesserae a uni-coloured area can become a space alive with light which will change as the viewer changes his position. It is said that the Byzantine mosaicists carefully set each individual tessera at the exact angle which would give the best reflection when viewed from the floor.

The careful planning of the directional 'flow' of the tesserae is another essential factor in creating dynamic vitality: by giving a row of tesserae a definite direction one increases tremendously the tension and rhythm of one area in relation to another: the contrast of areas of lively movement to areas of calm restfulness will give the mosaic a dynamic rhythm; this is particularly important in a large-scale mural. Fig. 11 is an analysis of the tesserae 'flow' on the mosaic shown in Plate 14.

The setting of tesserae at different angles and heights, the directional 'flow', etc., will be considered at greater length in Chapter 6 when we will discuss the methods of application. But you must give these problems sufficient thought at the planning stage and not wait until the execution of the mosaic.

If you use materials other than glass tesserae, consider their special qualities of size, surface texture and relative light reflecting qualities. By using areas of different kinds of materials next to each other you can add greatly to the interest of the mosaic. These potential variations are, of course, one of the

FIG II
Analysis of the 'flow' of the tesserae
on the mosaic shown in Plate 14

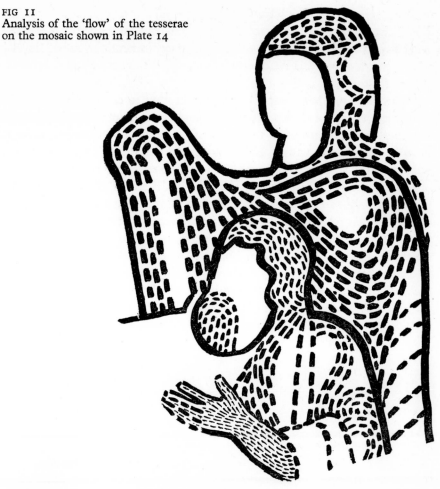

major differences between mosaic and painting, where you are relatively restricted in the use of textures and height differences and where reflection plays no part in the effect. In mosaics the possible combinations are vast: you can set glass tesserae against pieces of ceramic tile, shiny surfaces against dull materials like slate or stone, small pieces against large ones, etc.

The beginner who has no design experience but wants to create mosaics because the medium attracts him may be somewhat at a loss as to how to start his design and a few fundamental suggestions may help. Although it may not be absolutely necessary for the mosaicist to be an expert draughtsman, a feeling for spatial relationship, composition and colour is essential. Sensibility and awareness of these can be acquired through practice and experiment.

Base your first design on some natural form: a flower, a leaf, a fish, a bird, a butterfly, a pine cone, a tree, a ship. Since we do not aim at a realistic representation of the object start by making a few preliminary sketches to reduce the natural form to its essentials by simplification and abstraction, i.e. by leaving out all details and accidentals which have no important function in the structure of the object. Once you have reduced the object to its simplest form, start experimenting with the composition itself. This means exploring the relationship of shapes to each other, of colours, weights, tones and textures within a given space: this relationship can be calm or turbulent and exciting, the balance of the individual parts can be symmetric or asymmetric, the colours and textures can be contrasting or unified. By experimenting you will develop your awareness of these relationships and acquire eventually an instinctive feeling for them.

First decide on the elements of which you want to compose your design: draw them on coloured or painted paper and cut them out. Start by keeping the number of colours down to three or four, since it will thus be easier to keep the composition unified. Even at this stage you should have some idea of what materials you are going to use. Match the coloured paper with the colours of these materials. These cut-out elements can be fairly small, since at first you want only to explore the relationship of the individual parts to each other and their relationship to the over-all space. Not only do you save time by making your first drawings in a small size, but there is also the additional advantage that you are forced to consider the essentials of form and colour instead of being sidetracked by irrelevant details. Cut out a piece of paper for the background in the proportions of your final mosaic. This background can, of course, be any colour or texture you like. Put the cut-out elements of your design on the background and try different ways of grouping them within

FIG 12

the given size of the background paper. Fig. 12 shows how entirely different compositions can be produced by arranging identical design elements in four different ways. As you try various ways of laying out the units you may, of course, find that you want to make one or two of them larger or smaller, brighter or more subdued in colour, more or less lively in texture and lighter or darker in tonal value, in order to make the composition more interesting or better proportioned.

When you have finally found an arrangement which satisfies you as to the relationship of the different shapes and colours to each other and to the whole area, paste the various elements into position. You then have a simplified schematic composition on which you can base the final cartoon.

If you want to make a completely abstract design, follow a similar procedure: cut out shapes or self-contained units of little designs or patterns and again experiment with various combinations of colours, textures and sizes on different backgrounds until you have found a satisfactory arrangement.

When the basic composition has been settled you must enlarge the small schematic sketch into the proper cartoon. If the final mosaic will not be bigger than, say, 3 ×4 ft you can make the cartoon the same size. It is not practicable, especially for the beginner, to make a cartoon larger than this. Even for a very much larger mosaic or mural the cartoon should not be bigger, for only in this size can you easily judge the balance and correct relationship of the various parts in your composition. When the cartoon is completed you must enlarge it to the final mosaic size.

The easiest method of enlarging your small schematic sketch to the cartoon size is by 'squaring up'. Rule a grid of squares over your small sketch and number each square for easier orientation. Then divide the paper on which you want to draw the cartoon into the same number of squares: these will, of course, be proportionally larger. Number them in the same way as the small grid and copy the small sketch square by square on to the larger size. Do not attempt to enlarge the small schematic sketch simply by eye, since it is very

difficult to retain the exact proportions when transferring it to the larger size. It sounds easy enough, but it takes a great deal of experience and a well-trained eye to be able to do this.

Never do your cartoon on a table but always work on an easel or pin your paper on a wall. This will allow you to step back from your design and look at it from the distance from which the final mosaic will be viewed. I cannot stress the importance of this too much; it applies to all painting but even more so to designing a mosaic cartoon: the mosaic itself will usually be executed on a horizontal table and you will not be able to see the whole design until it has been completed.

When you have transferred the elements of your schematic design to the cartoon paper in simple outlines, you have the basic framework on which to start the painting of the actual cartoon. Redraw the whole design with bold strokes in charcoal, black felt-pen or paint applied as freely as possible with a fair-sized bristle brush to achieve that boldness and simplicity so necessary in mosaic design. Poster paint is a convenient paint to use; it is an opaque water-colour available in all shades which will enable you to match exactly the colour of the tesserae or other materials that you want to use. Keep the design bold and simple and do not under any circumstances try to imitate the final mosaic effect by trying to paint individual tesserae or pieces of stone (Plate 37). Aim at accuracy only in outlining the general shapes which make up your composition; texture and shading should develop naturally and organically during the process of actually setting the tesserae or stones on the base.

The directional flow of the tesserae should follow the direction of the brush strokes in your cartoon: a firm brush stroke will help enormously to achieve the necessary rhythm in the final mosaic. Obviously firmness of brush work will come only after a certain amount of practice; try to follow the natural flow of a garment, the construction of a building or the growth of a plant. In an abstract design which relies entirely on the tensions and rhythm of areas of colours, of shapes and lines, it is even more important that the flow of the tesserae should reinforce these tensions by following the contours of colour masses and shapes or by giving certain areas a strong directional pull (see Fig. 11).

Do not spoil your sketch by too many corrections; a degree of spontaneity is important and it is sometimes better to start again from scratch rather than to work too long on the same sketch. When you have completed the cartoon, put a piece of tracing paper over it and trace the outline of your design on it. Rub pencil graphite or crayon on to the back of the tracing with a piece of cotton wool and trace the design with a hard pencil or ball-point pen on to the base on which you are going to set your mosaic. If necessary, go over the outline with a felt-pen so that the strong outline remains visible when you start the spreading of the adhesive. If you are going to use expanded metal mesh on your base board (see Chapter 5) a strong outline is especially important to enable you to see it clearly through the mesh.

If your cartoon is smaller than the intended mosaic 'square up' as described above. The best though more expensive method of enlarging a cartoon is by getting a photostat made: a photostat will reproduce accurately all the subtleties and happy accidents of your cartoon; the liveliness of a line and the direction of the brush strokes will all be retained. There is no limit to the size of a photostat so that they can be used as a basis of even the largest murals.

If you want to make a large-scale mosaic or mural in your studio it will be necessary to divide the whole design into manageable sections. Their size will be determined by the weight of the material which you want to use (for example, each section of a mosaic made of glass tesserae on a concrete base should not be larger than about 3 ft by 4 ft). When dividing the design on your tracing paper or photostat do not divide it mechanically into rectangles but

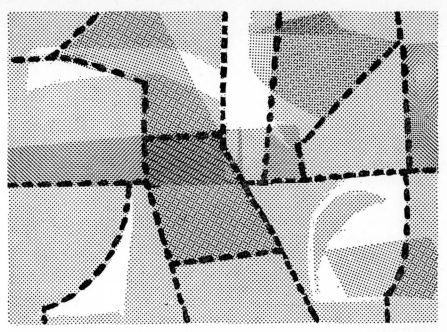

FIG 13 When dividing a large-scale design into sections let the outlines of the sections follow the main lines of the design

make a sort of jig-saw puzzle in which the outlines of the sections follow the main lines in your design (Fig. 13); cut along the outlines of self-contained areas wherever possible. This will make the seams of the assembled mosaic less noticeable and it will also increase its physical stability; the protrusions of one section will interlock with the recesses of the adjoining section, rather as in a large dove-tail joint.

Some experienced mosaicists do not work from a detailed cartoon but, especially if the mosaic is to be made *in situ*, scratch the design into the wet mortar after it has been applied to the wall. Obviously this method requires a great deal of experience and an ability to visualize the completed mosaic in one's mind.

5 Bases

The type of base on which the mosaic is set will be determined by three factors: the size of the mosaic, its situation (whether indoors or outdoors) and the type of adhesive or mortar used for fixing the tesserae or other materials.

Wood Base

Wood is the ideal base for indoor mosaics: it is easily available, reasonable in price and easy to saw into the desired size and shape. Ordinary plywood or the better grades of blockboard are suitable. The wood must be rigid, especially if it is to be more than 2 ft long. For smaller mosaics $\frac{1}{2}$ to $\frac{3}{4}$ in. thickness is adequate but for larger sizes at least $\frac{3}{4}$ in. thickness should be used. All wooden bases should be watersealed before you begin to set the tesserae. This will prevent warping and also allows the tesserae to stick firmly to the base if you use glues or mastics: untreated wood might soak up the moisture of the adhesive before bonding has taken place. Paint two coats of waterproofing sealer on both sides and all edges of the wood. Stand the wood upright and paint the two sides one immediately after the other to prevent the moisture content in the wood from warping the whole piece during the sealing process. This waterproof sealer is obtainable from builders' merchants or timber dealers.

Ordinary plywood should not be used for outdoor mosaics. Even the watersealing might not be enough to keep the wood from warping when it is directly exposed to the elements. For outdoor mosaics only marine-ply must be used. This is a superior and more expensive type of plywood in which the layers of wood are bonded together with a high-quality type of resin which will not allow any moisture to penetrate. The surface of the marine-ply needs no watersealing; but two coats of watersealing paint should be applied to all sawn edges and around any holes which have been drilled into it.

When the waterproof paint is thoroughly dry transfer your design on to the wood (as described in Chapter 4). A photostat copy which is glued to the base with a waterbased glue will stretch slightly. Therefore you should make the wooden base slightly larger than the dry photostat. Using a large brush, paint a good plastic glue on to the wood and the back of the photostat, allowing a few minutes for the moisture to penetrate the photographic paper so that it will stretch slightly. Starting with the upper edge of the photostat, lay it on to the wood. If air bubbles should be trapped between wood and paper, make an incision in the paper with a razor blade to allow the air to escape. When the paper dries it will shrink again and should adhere smoothly to the board without any crinkles. Since the tesserae or stones which you will fix to the photostat will be quite heavy, ensure that the photostat will stay permanently in position by nailing it to the wood with small copper or brass tacks, especially around the edges.

If the mosaic panel is to hang on a wall fix the hangers to the back of the wood base before setting the tesserae, to avoid damaging the completed mosaic. If the mosaic is to be fixed by means of bolts, drill holes which are slightly larger than the bolts. To keep the mortar or adhesive from running through these holes when you set the tesserae, plug them temporarily with wooden pegs or dowel-rods 2 in. high. Set the tesserae around them and remove the pegs when the mosaic is completed. After the bolts have secured the mosaic to the wall, cover the holes with the appropriate tesserae.

If you use cement mortar for setting the tesserae it will be necessary to fix expanded metal mesh (Fig. 14) to the wood or photostat to enable the mortar

FIG 14   Expanded metal mesh and shears

to adhere to the base. This mesh is available from builders' merchants and must be cut with metal shears to the exact size of the base board (Fig. 15). Lay the cut mesh on top of the wood on which you have drawn your design or on the photostat. (If you use metal mesh the photostat need not be glued to

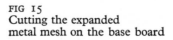

FIG 15
Cutting the expanded
metal mesh on the base board

the wood.) Fix the mesh with rust-resisting staples at intervals of at least 6 in. and of about 4 in. along the edges. To prevent the mortar from running away, nail 1½ in. strips of wood around the whole wooden base; they should protrude at least ¾ in. above the surface on which the tesserae will be laid.

For large-scale murals divide your sketch into sections as described above. Trace the outlines of the sections of the sketch or glue the photostat on to the board and saw the wood along the sectional outlines (Fig. 16). An electric jigsaw, bandsaw or scroll saw is almost indispensable; the blade of the saw has to be fairly thin so that you can follow the curves of the sections accurately. Accurate sawing is very important in order to avoid troublesome gaps when the mosaic is being finally assembled. If two adjoining sections can be obtained by sawing one large piece of wood in two, an accurate fit for the final assembly is automatically assured. But very large designs will need more than one piece of board. In this case, too, the sawing of the edges of two adjoining pieces should be done in one operation so as to ensure accurate joints without gaps. Put the two pieces of wood on top of each other, overlapping them to such an extent that a double thickness of wood covers the whole of the intended joint.

FIG 16   Sawing the base board of a large-scale mosaic into sections with an electrical jigsaw

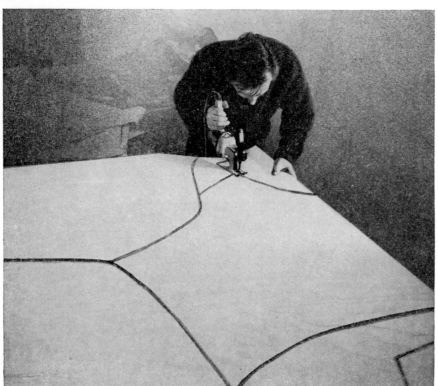

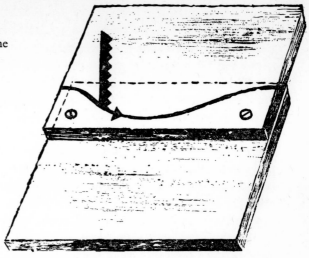

FIG 17 Sawing through two adjoining pieces of wood in one operation to obtain a perfect joint between them

Screw the two pieces of wood provisionally together so that they cannot move when you saw them. Saw through the two layers of wood and remove the provisional screws (Fig. 17).

After watersealing the sawn edges as described on page 70 you should nail strips of wood $1\frac{1}{2}$ in. wide along all the straight edges of the different sections. For the curved edges you must use a thin, flexible material to which the mortar will not adhere. Strips of strong celluloid are suitable. They are easily cut and are then nailed to the edges. When setting the tesserae, always fit two adjoining sections of the base together, separated only by these strips of celluloid. This enables you to work on the two sections as if they were one: thus the flow of the design and tesserae can continue uninterrupted from one section into the other and you can practically ignore the joint (Fig. 18). The strip of celluloid will prevent the mortar from joining the two sections permanently and is removed after the mortar has dried. As a further insurance against the joints between sections being visible after reassembly of the mosaic, leave out a tessera or stone here and there on either side of the separation line. After the mosaic has been permanently installed *in situ*, you can insert the missing tesserae or stones right across the separation line and in this way help to obliterate it.

FIG 18 When setting tesserae on two adjoining pieces of wood, ignore the joint between them so that the 'flow' of the tesserae continues naturally from one piece into the other

Concrete Bases

Reinforced concrete sounds an overwhelming material. One thinks of building sites where labourers with spades and cement mixers get down to work without having to worry about the mess they make. But actually you can use it quite easily in your studio; apart from a certain amount of dust it need not create too much of a mess unless you break a cement bag (in spite of its weight cement is packed in paper bags).

Concrete is the most suitable material for all outdoor uses. It is weatherproof and extremely durable. It is cheaper than all other materials; this can be quite an important consideration if the mosaic or mural is a large-scale one. The main disadvantage is its considerable weight. A mosaic laid on a concrete base measuring more than about 3 to 4 ft square cannot be lifted comfortably. For any larger sizes you have to work in sections. Begin by constructing a form the size of the final mosaic (or mosaic section in the case of a large-scale work) into which the concrete will be poured. This form consists of a piece of plywood (any thickness will do) to which a wooden frame at least 3 in. high is nailed. For easier separation of the dried concrete slab from the wooden form, apply some grease to the parts of the wood which will come into contact with the concrete.

MIXING Do not mix the concrete in too cold a room; and obviously frost will ruin the wet concrete. About 10° C. (50° F.) is the lowest temperature in which you should work, otherwise the concrete will not set properly. The raw materials for making a precast concrete base are all available from builders' merchants. The mixture should consist of one part cement, two parts sand and three parts aggregate (usually crushed rock) to which water is added. (The aggregate should not be too coarse and should pass through a mesh no wider than $\frac{3}{8}$ in.) The most important point about preparing concrete is the thorough mixing of the ingredients: each particle of sand and aggregate should be completely coated with cement paste to give it the desired structural strength. First mix the dry ingredients thoroughly with a trowel and then slowly add water until the compound has reached the consistency of dough. If too much water is used the hardened concrete will be structurally weak: the drier the mixture, the more durable the final product will be.

INGREDIENTS The most suitable cement is ordinary Portland cement (which is not a trade name but is so called because it resembles Portland stone in its grey colour and durability). This is available in bags of from 7 to 94 pounds. If it has been stored for some time, moisture in the air may have caused parts of the cement to coagulate into little lumps. In order to obtain a thoroughly mixed concrete you should sift the cement through a finely meshed sieve.

Pour the concrete mixture evenly to a thickness of $\frac{1}{2}$ in. into the wooden form which you have prepared, pressing it well into the corners with a small trowel or spatula (Figs. 19 and 20). To reinforce the concrete, place a 3 in. or 4 in. reinforcing mesh on the concrete. This mesh should be cut slightly smaller than the inside of the form since it must not touch the sides of the wood. When the mesh has been laid in position, pour a second layer of con-

FIG 19   Trowel

FIG 20   Palette knife

crete mixture to cover the mesh. After a few hours the concrete will begin to set and at that moment you should roughen the surface by scratching crossed lines all over it. This is important, so that the 'setting bed' into which you set the tesserae will get a good grip or 'key' on the concrete base.

You must ensure that the curing of the concrete takes place very gradually. The concrete shrinks slightly while it is drying and so cracks might form. This can be avoided if the concrete is kept moist for a week or at least several days by frequently sprinkling it with water and covering it with wet newspaper, cloth or sacks at night. When the concrete has cured and dried remove the wooden form, and the concrete bed is now ready to receive the 'setting bed' of cement mortar.

Wood and concrete are the most suitable bases for laying the tesserae in the direct method (see Chapter 6), but other materials can be used: metals which are rustproof (e.g. aluminium which is, however, expensive) or metals which have been carefully painted with anti-corrosive paint; asbestos, cement sheets (which are cheap and available to a thickness of 1 in.) and synthetic resins reinforced with glass fibre which you can further reinforce with metal rods for very large bases. Another cheap and weather-resistance material is Tempered Masonite: this is a type of hardboard, available in all thicknesses. All the edges and drilled holes should be watersealed as in wood. More expensive substances such as plate glass, Perspex or Formica can be used to great effect if only part of the panel is to be covered with mosaic and certain parts of the base itself remain visible.

6 Adhesives and methods of application

There are two fundamentally different methods of setting tesserae and other materials on to the base: the direct method and the reverse method. In the direct method each stone or piece of material is fixed directly to the base with an adhesive or embedded into a mortar. This was the only method used until the decline of the mosaic during the Renaissance; the ancient Greek, Roman and Byzantine mosaics were all done by setting the tesserae or stones into various types of mortar. But when mosaic workshops were set up in Italy during the Renaissance and the making of mosaics became a commercialized industry, the reverse method became generally accepted. In this method a mirror image of the design is traced on to a piece of strong paper; on this the

FIG 21   Reverse method: pasting the tesserae on paper

tesserae are pasted, upside down, with a water-soluble paste or gum (Fig. 21). When the mosaic has been completed in this manner, the whole sheet of paper with the glued-on tesserae is lifted up and pressed into a bed of wet mortar. When the mortar has set hard the paper is wetted and peeled off. By this method the whole mosaic can be completed in the studio; mosaics covering entire walls and ceilings are made by dividing the whole design into small sections and embedding the completed mosaic sections into the mortar. These small sheets of paper with the mounted tesserae are much easier to transport than the much heavier panels done in the direct method. In Italian workshops decorations of whole churches are manufactured in this manner and sent in crates to all parts of the world, together with exact plans for fixing them in position. For instance, the mosaic decorations for the Blessed Sacrament Chapel in Westminster Cathedral in London were assembled in the Orsoni workshops in Venice from designs made in the Paris studio of Boris Anrep and then sent to London for fixing on the walls and ceilings of the Cathedral.

In classical and Byzantine times labour presented no problem, but today it is often not practicable to set the tesserae for a large project *in situ*: mosaicists working on scaffolding to reach parts of a building which are not easily accessible, the hoisting up of a great number of boxes with the different tesserae and similar physical problems could make the cost quite prohibitive.

By using the reverse method any mistakes in the setting of the tesserae or in the design can be easily corrected by removing the tesserae from the paper; the removal of portions of mosaic which have been fixed by the direct method might mean damaging the base or at least hard physical exertion, especially if cement mortar has been used.

The reverse method is also appropriate if a smooth mosaic surface is desired. Since the exposed side of the tesserae will be the one which had been glued to the paper the surface will be smooth and even without protrusions or recesses. For functional objects like table tops this is essential. It might also be advisable for some outside murals which are very exposed to the elements, since rain water should not be allowed to collect on the mosaic.

But having enumerated all the advantages of the reverse method I want to stress very emphatically that, in my opinion, the direct method is artistically far superior. A certain mechanical finish is unavoidable in the reverse method. The main advantage of the direct method is that you can see and control the final effect whilst working. You can achieve subtle effects quite impossible in the reverse method: in particular, only in the direct method can you vary the angle and height at which you set the tesserae. Only thus can you create the exact texture and light reflection you desire; lively texture and the controlled play of light on the tesserae are, after all, two of the most attractive features of mosaics, especially if you use glass material. The bas-relief type or three-dimensional mosaic in which certain portions are raised above the rest can be done with any degree of finesse only in the direct method. I have seen in some Italian workshops an artificial method of creating uneven surface textures in reverse mosaics: the tool used is a wooden board into which a dozen or so nails have been fixed so that they protrude by about 1 in. After the tesserae have been embedded into the mortar these nails are pressed on to the mosaic surface, thereby pushing a few tesserae deeper into the soft mortar which creates a certain unevenness of texture. Obviously, I do not recommend such mechanical short cuts to achieve effects which convince no one.

Direct Method

It is impossible to lay down any rigid rules for the use of glues, mastics and mortars; with experience every mosaicist will choose the type of adhesive or mortar best suited to his working methods and particular designs.

The beginner is advised to use ready-mixed mastics and glues. For small indoor panels which require a considerable amount of detailed work the use of glue is advisable; it allows the tesserae to be set closely together, since each tessera is simply pasted on to the base. On the other hand, when using mastic or mortar a small crevice has to be left between the tesserae to allow the adhesive to surround each tessera for firm adhesion.

For larger and outdoor projects cement mortar or water-proof tile adhesive should be used; outdoor mosaics will usually be viewed from a fair distance and not a great deal of detailed work will be necessary. Mortar or mastic must also be used when you want to set the material at varying angles or heights or to make a bas-relief type of mosaic.

GLUES, MASTICS AND PLASTIC ADHESIVES   A great variety of PVA-based glues are available at most hardware shops. They are sold under different trade names and all those whose directions mention adhesion to glass are suitable. Most PVA glues are colourless. Rubber-based compounds are usually black or off-white. Where this does not present any problems as far as the design is concerned, they are a good if slightly messy material to use; their power of adhesion is excellent. A plastic adhesive has been developed in Italy specially for glass tesserae mosaic; details of this are given in Chapter 7 (page 92).

'Mastic' meant originally an organic gum resin used in the manufacture of tile adhesives, but the word is used more loosely today and includes many man-made compounds. Tile merchants sell a great variety of tile mastic adhesives with varying properties, details of which are found on page 92.

METHODS OF APPLICATION   Choose an area of your design of a size which you can cover comfortably before the adhesive sets hard. This will depend on the speed at which you work and the type of adhesive you have chosen. A beginner should start with a small area at a time so as to get the feel of the material. This area should be a self-contained, logical unit of the design. With a palette knife or spatula (Fig. 20) spread the adhesive evenly on to this unit and set the tesserae one by one in rows, starting with the contour of the chosen area (Fig. 22). Make sure that each tessera or piece of stone is held

FIG 22   When setting the tesserae start with the contours. Printers' 'furniture' is used to wall in a particular area of the design

firmly in place by pressing it down, but do not allow the adhesive to be squeezed up above the surface of the tesserae. Complete the whole contour of the area first and then fill in the inside area. Pay particular attention to the 'flow' of the tesserae. If you use rectangular smalti this flow will be achieved automatically if you set the tesserae in rows with their small sides touching each other. But even a row of square tesserae will subtly reflect the physical action of setting them and the direction in which you have worked. The tessera flow will enhance the form of each shape and set off one area dynamically against another (Fig. 11). The tension set up by the contrasting flow of tesserae varying from one area to another cannot be stressed enough: without it your mosaic might resemble a tiled bathroom wall and will lack interest and movement. Study your cartoon for the direction in which the tesserae should flow, because only by studying the whole design can you decide the required flow of a particular group of tesserae. When working on a small area there is always a danger that you may get so engrossed in details that you will forget to consider the work as a complete composition. The direction of the flow of tesserae should follow the direction of the brush strokes on your cartoon. Whenever you have completed a particular area and allowed it to dry sufficiently to prevent the tesserae from sliding down, put the mosaic upright against a wall so that you can step back and look at the general effect. This will also help you to gauge the light reflection of tesserae and tiles on the mosaic once it has been installed in its permanent position; light reflection of a vertical mosaic will obviously be quite different from the mosaic lying on your horizontal work table. If you set your tesserae at different heights the light colours should be raised above the dark ones and strong colours above neutral shades in order to give them additional emphasis.

If an area requires a great deal of detailed work, progress will be correspondingly slower. In this case it is advisable to 'butter' each tessera individually with adhesive instead of spreading it over a whole area on the base. This has the additional advantage that you can see the details of your drawing, which gets covered if you spread adhesive over a whole area. For buttering, hold each tessera between two fingers and spread the adhesive on to it with a palette knife. Another method is to put a blob of adhesive on a saucer and dip each tessera into it so that it picks up enough adhesive to bond it firmly to the base.

If you use glue or mastic for an indoor mosaic it is not necessary to 'grout' it, i.e. fill the crevices between tesserae or tiles with cement. The adhesive should be enough to hold the tesserae securely in place; the gaps between the stones are part of the lively texture of the mosaic and should be used creatively to bring out the direction of the flow of tesserae and to help to define the form of each part of your design. Grouting, however, will be necessary for outdoor mosaics to prevent water from settling in the crevices. Ready-mixed waterproof cement grout is available from tiling merchants. If you want to make your own grouting mixture add one part of hydrated lime to six parts of white or grey Portland cement and cement colour as required. Thoroughly mix the dry ingredients and add water until the mixture has reached the consistency of thin porridge. Spread this into the crevices and wipe off the surplus with a damp cloth. Allow the grout to dry for 24 hours.

CEMENT MORTAR Notwithstanding the many new plastic cements and adhesives which are on the market today, mortar made from cement, sand, 'aged' lime and water is still in many respects the best material in which to set your tesserae, tiles or stone.

It is the cheapest of all the materials mentioned so far and its durability has been proved beyond doubt; after all, many of the mosaics set in cement mortar by the Romans over 2,000 years ago are still in excellent condition today. As a material it has a nice feel to it; it responds well to creative shaping; its sculptural quality enables you to vary the angle and height at which you set each tessera or stone; and it is the most suitable material for making a bas-relief mosaic. Its adhesive properties are excellent and it is the ideal medium for setting materials of different thicknesses on one mosaic; for instance, glass tesserae and thick stone can both be embedded in the cement mortar to the same surface level if you so desire. It can be applied directly to a concrete base (which should, however, be thoroughly wetted before the cement mortar is applied so that the concrete will not soak up the moisture in the mortar). On all other bases expanded metal mesh must be fixed so that the mortar can get a firm grip. Its disadvantage is its weight; a mosaic set in cement mortar on a concrete base should not exceed about 12 sq ft; the size of mosaics set on other types of base will be governed by the weight and rigidity of the base material.

The recipe for mixing the cement mortar for setting the tesserae gives a somewhat richer mixture than the recipe for making the base given on page 74 since greater plasticity for easier working and smoother texture is required. There are as many recipes for mixing the cement mortar as there are artists working with it; with experience you will arrive at a mixture most suited to your special needs. I have found these proportions to be the most successful ones: four parts (by volume) of cement, three parts of sand and one part of 'aged' lime and cement dye as required. There is quite a bit of latitude in the proportions of the ingredients, but thorough mixing and slow curing are most important. All the ingredients mentioned are available at most builders' merchants.

CEMENT Portland cement as described on page 74 is also suitable for making the cement mortar for the setting bed.

SAND Different grades of coarseness are available. As a beginner you should use the finest grain available since it is easier to work with, especially on small mosaics.

HYDRATED LIME The purpose of using lime is to bind the cement and sand into a more plastic mixture, thereby making the mortar easier and more agreeable to work with. It also slows down the hardening process and reduces the shrinkage of the mortar as it hardens. The lime should be 'aged' by mixing it with water several days before you want to use it. Always have a certain amount of lime prepared so that you can start work whenever you wish. Mix the hydrated lime and water in a plastic bucket to the thickness of cream and leave to settle. After some hours pour off any surplus water which may have appeared on top of your mixture. In a few days' time the lime will have the consistency of dough and will be ready for use. It does no harm to the quality of the lime if, after a further period of time, it dries to a chalk-like substance. You must not stir water into it again since that would destroy its binding power; to use it, simply crumble it to a fine powder in your hands.

CEMENT COLOUR   Cement ranges in colour from white to grey. Where it is visible in the crevices between the tesserae it should not be too light in colour because that will disrupt the general effect of your design and also 'drain' the brightness of the colours of the tesserae. A neutral darkish grey is less obtrusive and therefore less disturbing to the over-all effect; it encloses, as it were, each tessera in a dark frame, increasing the brilliance of its colour. On the other hand the effect of the grey on a neutral background shade will be one of unification and this, in turn, will bring out the rhythm of areas of exciting colour and calmer background.

Black weatherproof cement dyes are sold at builders' merchants under various trade names. They are also available in various colours but these should be used only for special effects and with great restraint; the mortar should set off the coloured tesserae or tiles, not compete with them. A mortar of the same colour as the tesserae will deaden the general effect, and the mosaic will lose a lot of its sparkle, which is one of its most exciting qualities.

APPLYING THE MORTAR AND SETTING THE TESSERAE   Make a heap of the mortar ingredients (see page 80) on a slab of plate glass or marble (for easy cleaning). Mix them very thoroughly with a trowel before adding any water. Then form a little crater in the centre of the heap and pour water into it very gradually, allowing it to soak into the mixture. Then add more water and mix until the consistency of dough has been reached. You should not make the mixture too liquid: mortar made with too much water will be structurally weak when it has hardened. In any case, it is easier to set the tesserae in a fairly stiff mixture, and also the shrinkage in a dry mix is less than in a very moist one; you can add more water if the mixture becomes too dry through evaporation whilst you are working.

Choose an area of approximately 6 in. square on your design, which is the amount of space you can comfortably cover before the concrete becomes too dry. As I mentioned earlier, the area chosen should be a self-contained and natural unit of your design. To prevent the mortar mixture from running and spreading beyond the desired area, I have found printers' 'furniture' useful (Fig. 22). These are strips of lead alloy which you can acquire from practically any printer. They are heavy enough to prevent the mortar from pushing them aside, are available in various lengths and can easily be broken into shorter pieces. Form these metal strips into a miniature wall surrounding the area which you want to cover with mortar. If the base has been covered with expanded metal mesh (see page 71) work the mortar well into the mesh with a trowel or, for awkward corners, a palette knife.

If the mortar is applied to a concrete base it is essential to moisten the base thoroughly before applying the mortar. If you fail to do this the dry concrete base will act like blotting paper and soak up the moisture from the mortar, thus destroying its binding power. After you have wetted the concrete base, paint a thin mixture of cement and water on to it with a large brush just before spreading the cement mortar. It is interesting to note that the reason why parts of the old Byzantine mosaics have become detached is not that inferior cement was used in them but that the mortar did not adhere to the first layer of cement or plaster.

The thickness of the mortar will be determined by the thickness of the material which you want to set; when you press the tesserae or tiles firmly into the mortar they should protrude slightly above the level of the mortar bed. If they sink below it, this means that you have spread the mortar too thickly or made the mixture too liquid. If you use ceramic tiles it is important to immerse them in water for several minutes before setting them. The unglazed parts of a tile are very porous and unless you soak them first they will absorb water from the mortar, which will prevent the bonding of the two.

When you have covered the whole walled-in area with tesserae or whatever material you are using, wait until the mortar has hardened sufficiently to enable you to remove the metal strips without the mortar and tesserae shifting. This will take one or two hours, depending on the humidity and temperature of your studio. Then repeat the process, walling-in an adjoining area with printers' metal strips and covering it with mortar. It is important that the completed area to which you join the new one should again be quite moist. If some time has elapsed between work on the two areas, thoroughly moisten the completed area before laying down the new mortar. As I emphasized in the chapter on bases, cement mortar must be allowed to cure very slowly and should be kept moist from several days to a week. Cover it with wet newspaper, cloth or sacks at night or use plastic sheeting to prevent evaporation.

After the last completed area has been allowed to cure in this manner you can apply the grouting mixture if it is required (see page 79).

If you apply the cement mortar to an existing surface such as a wall, the surface must be roughened with a chisel to allow the mortar to key properly. Here, too, the surface must be thoroughly wetted and painted over with a thin cement and water mixture before applying the mortar. Work with as dry a mortar mixture as possible and start work at the bottom so as to prevent the mortar from sliding down. It is important to work the mortar well into the roughened surface with a trowel to ensure a good grip.

A very strong cement mortar is obtained by the addition of a bonding agent to the cement mixture or by mixing Portland cement only with the bonding agent. A variety of such plastic bonding agents are available from builders' merchants. This is an especially suitable mixture for setting mosaic directly on to a vertical wall. The bonding agent and cement are mixed with water to a dough-like consistency; the working methods are the same as described for ordinary cement mortar.

When the mosaic has set hard you reach the thrilling moment when, as you clean the surface, the brilliant tesserae begin to appear out of the grey cement mess. First scrub the mosaic with a dry wire brush which will remove most of the surplus mortar from the surface of the tesserae. Then mix a solution of water and 10 per cent hydrochloric acid or muriatic acid in a glass bowl (not metal) and, dipping a small stiff brush into the solution, clean off the remaining bits of mortar, giving special attention to little corners and ridges. Hydrochloric acid is a vicious chemical and you must wear rubber gloves for this operation and be careful not to spill any on your clothing. Always add the acid to the water, not the other way around. Finally wash the whole surface with clean warm water (do not add any detergent) and polish with a dry cloth.

Reverse Method

ADHESIVES AND CEMENT MORTAR As mentioned briefly on page 76, in the reverse method the tesserae, etc., are pasted on to paper or cloth upside down; the completed mosaic is then embedded into cement mortar or adhesive which has been applied to the base on which the mosaic is to be set.

Draw the design in reverse on thick brown paper or use a photostat which you can order in reverse from the photographer. If you have to divide the design into sections for a large-scale project cut sections of 2 to 3 ft square. Before cutting the paper into sections you should draw large squiggles with

FIG 23 Reverse method: draw large squiggles on the back of the paper as register marks. Number each section

FIG 24 Reverse method: after thoroughly wetting the backing paper, strip it off

a black felt pen on the back of the paper or photostat (Fig. 23). These squiggles will act as register marks and enable you to fit the sections accurately together when you press the tesserae mounted on the paper into the cement or mastic. Also number the sections consecutively and mark your original cartoon with corresponding numbers for easier reference.

The paste with which you stick the tesserae to the paper must be both strong and water-soluble so that the paper can be peeled off easily when the mosaic has been set into the mortar or adhesive. The two most commonly used pastes are water and flour or water and gum arabic. For the flour paste you mix one part of flour with six parts of water and boil the mixture. Gum arabic is available as a liquid from artists' supply shops, or you can obtain gum arabic crystals from a chemist or drug store and dissolve them in hot water.

Fix the tesserae to the paper either by brushing the paste on to the tesserae or by covering an area of the paper with the paste and sticking the tesserae on to it (page 76). They should be set close together, but small gaps must be left between the tesserae so that the wet setting mortar or adhesive can squeeze up into the gaps and hold each tessera in place when the completed mosaic is pressed into its setting bed. For this reason do not use too much paste when sticking the tesserae on the paper since that would fill up these small gaps; there should be just enough paste to hold each tessera in place. But press them down firmly on to the paper since each sheet will have to stand quite a lot of handling before it is finally embedded in the mortar. Allow the completed sheet to dry for at least a day before handling it.

When all the sheets have dried completely, mark the exact position of each sheet on the base or wall on which you want to fix the mosaic. Spread a layer of adhesive or cement mortar to about half the thickness of the tesserae. Then spread a very thin layer on top of the tesserae on the paper, working it carefully into the crevices with a small trowel. With the help of an assistant, now place a sheet with the mosaic on the base or wall, with the paper uppermost, and press down gently so that the two layers of adhesive or mortar become one. Tap the paper gently with a flat piece of wood to give the mosaic an even surface. Allow the mortar or adhesive to dry for a few hours. It should be firm but should not have set completely because after removing the paper you want to be able to make small corrections and adjustments to the tesserae; this must be done before the setting bed has hardened completely. When this state of semi-hardness has been reached wet the paper thoroughly by going over it a few times with a big brush or sponge dipped in warm water. Allow the water enough time to dissolve the paste with which you have pasted the tesserae on to the paper and then carefully strip off the paper (Fig. 24). Now make any necessary adjustments to tesserae which may have moved and very carefully remove any particles of adhesive or mortar which may have appeared on the surface of the tesserae; but do not clean the mosaic properly yet since this might dislodge parts of it. That should be done only after the setting bed has dried completely. If you have used cement mortar, allow it to cure slowly by splashing water on to it frequently with a large brush and putting wet newspaper over it during the night to slow down the drying process.

The setting of a mosaic into a vertical cement mortar bed needs quite a bit of practice, especially if you have to set a large mosaic into a cement mortar on a wall; in such a case you would be well advised to call in an expert tile setter. The moisture content of the setting bed must be 100 per cent correct: on the one hand it has to have the proper adhesive properties, and on the other hand it must not be too moist since this might cause the whole mosaic to slide down. Without the necessary experience you might easily ruin a work which may have taken several weeks to complete. Expert tile setters have the necessary knowledge and the extra cost is usually very worth while for any major projects.

GLASS PLASTICS Glass plastics is a combination of two materials: glass fibre and synthetic resin. Glass fibre alone lacks rigidity, and synthetic resins lack structural strength, but the combination of the two makes a material of tremendous strength. The main advantage of glass plastics over cement mixtures is its lightness. It is an inexpensive material, especially if you buy it in fairly large quantities, although the resins must not be stored too long before use. The stickiness of the resins make glass plastics a rather messy material to work with. Good ventilation in your studio is essential, since the curing agents are very volatile and give off unpleasant fumes. You must protect your skin with a suitable barrier cream since synthetic resins affect the skin rapidly. However, once you have mastered the use of the glass plastics it is a very useful material.

Of the cold-setting synthetic resins, polyester and epoxy resins are the most suitable for use as a setting bed for mosaic. Epoxy has somewhat greater adhesive properties, polyester is somewhat easier to use. Both resins are composed from two liquid ingredients: the resin and the curing agent. When mixed together, the two liquids are transformed into a jelly-like substance, which finally hardens into a tough solid. This process is entirely chemical and the heat required to solidify the two ingredients is produced by an internal chemical reaction once they have been mixed. The time which will elapse between the mixing of the two ingredients and the completion of the hardening process is known as the 'pot life', and this process, once started, cannot be reversed. The pot life will vary according to the room temperature and the ingredients used, but the mixture must be applied during this comparatively short period of an hour or two. In general the higher the room temperature, the shorter the pot life will be. But the temperature in which the setting takes place should not be below 16° C. (60° F.), although winter additives are available where working under colder conditions is unavoidable. It is essential that the correct proportions of resin and curing agent should be used, since otherwise too much heat might be generated and the mixture might become too hot to handle and start fuming. But no such danger exists if the instructions of the manufacturers are followed correctly.

The mosaic is pasted on paper as described on page 84. Then construct a mould by cutting a piece of plywood to the exact size of the final mosaic, surrounding it with a 1 in. wooden frame. Cover the inside of this mould with paper in order to prevent the resin from adhering to the wood. Place the paper, with the mosaic uppermost, inside the wooden mould. Cut a piece of woven glass fibre and lay it on the mosaic to cover it completely.

The resin and the curing agent are then mixed, following the instructions of the manufacturers. Use a polythene bucket for the mixing since polythene is the only material to which the resins will not stick permanently. Pour the resin mixture to a thickness of about $\frac{1}{4}$ in. and allow it to set. The sequence of setting is a fairly sudden gelling, followed by a hardening stage during which the surface will remain tacky for a day or two. This in turn is followed by the hard setting known as polymerization, which might take as long as several weeks. But it is not necessary to wait until complete polymerization has taken place before the paper is removed from the mosaic. When the resin has lost its tackiness you can remove the whole mosaic from the mould, turn it upside down and remove the paper as described on page 84.

If the resin setting bed is to be poured on to a concrete base, it is important to neutralize the alkaline surface of the concrete, since the chemical reaction of the alkali might prevent good adhesion of the resin to the concrete. The concrete base should be thoroughly soaked with an etching solution of 10 per cent hydrochloric acid and water. This acid should be allowed to react for at least five minutes and should then be washed off with clean water. The concrete must be allowed to dry completely before the resin mixture is poured on to it. For maximum adhesion the concrete base should have a rough surface. The mixture of resin and curing agent is poured on to the concrete and the mosaic on the paper is pressed into it. After the resin has hardened remove the paper.

Double Reverse Method

When I discussed the advantages and disadvantages of the reverse and direct methods at the beginning of this chapter, I pointed out that a mosaic done in the reverse method will have a smooth surface since the tesserae are pasted down on the flat surface of the paper. This can, however, be overcome by reversing the reverse method. This is a somewhat cumbersome process but it is one way of retaining both the light weight of glass plastics and the advantages of texture and height variations possible in the direct method. Set the tesserae into very fine moist sand which has a certain degree of firmness without holding the tesserae permanently. Make a wooden form with a 1 in. frame around it and fill this box with a layer of fine sand which is thoroughly moistened. Set the tesserae in the same way as you would in the direct method, varying angles and height exactly as desired. When the mosaic has been completed, pour a thick layer of boiled fish glue over the whole mosaic and allow it to harden for at least a day. Then turn the whole arrangement over very carefully and remove the wooden form. Wash off the sand and make sure that none remains in the crevices between the tesserae. Then allow the mosaic to dry; this is most important since the synthetic resin will not harden if the mosaic is not completely free from moisture. Follow the procedure of laying the glass fibre and pouring the resin mixture as described above. Make sure that the tesserae are completely covered by the resin.

Mosaic Floors

The most suitable materials are marble, pebbles of different colours and sizes and unglazed ceramic tiles or tesserae. Glass tesserae can also be used if, after completion, the mosaic surface is polished to a smooth finish with a terrazzo machine.

In principle the methods of making a floor mosaic are the same as the direct or reverse methods of making mosaic murals. Since a floor has to be walked on, the greatest care has to be taken that the mosaic material is firmly embedded in the mortar. Whichever method is used a sound foundation is essential. This should consist of a thick concrete bed made of one part cement and three parts sand. The pouring of a large concrete area is not easy and the beginner should get professional assistance. When the foundation is properly cured pour a setting bed of one part cement and two or three parts of sand to which aged lime and a quantity of bonding agent (see page 82) has been added to ensure proper adhesion of the mosaic material to the mortar. Pour only an area which you can cover comfortably before the mortar begins to set. Press the stones or tesserae firmly into the mortar.

The floor can also be assembled by fitting prepared mosaic slabs together; these sections can be made in the direct or reverse method, depending on the intricacy of the design. The completed concrete slabs are embedded into a cement mortar which is poured on to the foundation. For good adhesion thoroughly moisten the slabs before laying them.

Translucent Mosaics

I should like to mention a type of mosaic somewhat outside the traditional type which we have discussed so far: the translucent mosaic.

With the invention of efficient transparent epoxy resins it became possible to create stained glass windows and panels without the laborious technique of holding each piece of glass in place by pieces of lead as used for the creation of glass windows since medieval times. Epoxy resins are both completely transparent and extremely durable and it is now possible to cut pieces of stained glass into tesserae of the desired size and simply glue them on a base of clear glass. Plate 27 shows an example of this type of work which reduces considerably the labour and cost of making a stained glass window. The window can be made by fitting the cut pieces of little regular or irregular squares of glass together to build up the design, or several layers of glass can be glued one on top of the other to give special colour effects. The whole can then be covered with a pane of clear glass to prevent dust from settling on the edges of the glass tesserae. It is important to allow a free flow of air between the two layers of plain glass in order to prevent condensation of moisture.

To be able to see the exact colour effects of the glass, work on a special work table which has a frosted glass top lit from below by a strip light which produces true 'daylight' and does not affect the shades of the different colours.

Paper Mosaics

In cases where the cost of the material would make it impossible for children to engage in the absorbing activity of mosaic making, paper is an excellent substitute. Plate 36 shows two boys of the University College School in London at work on a paper mosaic mural. Before the actual work begins 'tesserae' are made by painting sheets of paper in all the required shades in poster paint and cutting or tearing them to the required size. They should be sorted into boxes, according to colours.

7 The mosaic studio

The most important aspect of the studio for the professional mosaicist is its size; the materials which he uses are bulky – wood, bags of cement and sand, a selection of different coloured smalti and vitreous glass mosaic, materials like marble and stone, take up a great deal of space. Mosaics will usually be murals of a fair size; although they will probably be made in sections it is useful to be able to assemble as many sections as possible to gauge the effect of the complete mosaic. Ideally, the studio should measure at least 20 ft by 20 ft. It should contain a large sink and running water.

Mosaic making is a messy business. When cutting tesserae or stone, chips fly about and lie on the floor; cement, wet mortar or drops of hydrochloric acid are spilled. It is therefore important that the floor of the studio is both tough and easily cleaned. Good lighting is another essential requirement; since you will do a fair amount of your work on a horizontal worktable a studio skylight is not the ideal form of lighting, since the glass tesserae will reflect the top light into your eyes. The best source of light is a north window. This will ensure a diffused light without shadows. Direct sunlight on work must be shut out by blinds. Fluorescent strip lighting is an excellent way o lighting a studio, both in addition to daylight and after darkness. Fluorescent tubes should be fixed close to the ceiling to help the diffusion of the light. It is important to choose one of the many 'daylight' types on the market so that the colours of the materials are not changed.

The mosaic materials should be stored on shelves fixed to the walls. The different shades of smalti and vitreous glass mosaic are best kept in boxes. On each box paste a sample of the tesserae it contains so that each colour can

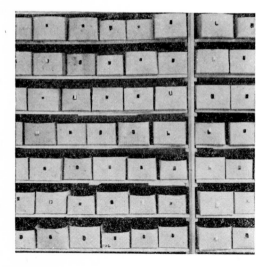

FIG 25 Paste one sample on each box of tesserae for easy identification of the colours

be found easily (Fig. 25). On other shelves stone, marble, etc., will be stored. If you use sheets of stained glass, construct a separate rack for each colour.

On one wall of your studio a board of plywood or composition material should be fixed. On this board you can pin the paper on which you will design your cartoon. There should be a fair amount of space in front of it so that you can step back from your design to view it from the greatest possible distance. The board should be as large as possible and be at right angles to the window for the best lighting.

The work table should be at least 6 ft long. It should be free-standing so that you can easily work on your mosaic from all sides. If you expect to execute large works such as murals a table made from planks put across two or three carpenter's trestles is useful.

A separate table should be reserved for making sketches. You will need a drawing board of about 2 ft by 3 ft, a T-square, a large set square, a 3-ft iron rule, compass, dividers, brushes, pots of poster paint and an easel.

If your workshop is large enough it is useful to fix an additional table 4 to 6 ft long to a wall. You also need a workbench with a vice for your woodwork. Above it fix a tool rack to the wall. It should hold all your woodworking tools, hammers, pincers, scraping tools and all your special mosaic tools and cutting instruments. You will have to do most of your mosaic work standing up, but for detailed work a stool which can be raised to the required height is a great help. And finally: a large polythene dustbin or wastebasket will enable you to dispose easily of such things as wet mortar and dangerous pieces of glass. An extraction fan with hood to collect dust and extract fumes could be useful.

Available materials and list of suppliers:

SMALTI

Smalti are sold by weight and approximately 3 lb will cover one square foot. Prices range in decreasing order according to colour groups. In Great Britain they are available from:

EDGAR UDNY AND CO LTD: 83 Bondway, Vauxhall, London SW 8
Mosley Road, Trafford Park, Manchester 17 and 6-8 Tomb Street, Belfast
Ordinary Gold
Ordinary Silver
Imperial Colours (reds, oranges and yellows)
Flesh Colours (flesh tints, light to dark)
Fine Colours (pure white, greens and blues)
Ordinary Colours (black, greys, browns, dark yellows, greens, blues, off-whites)
A sample card showing the available smalti can be obtained.

In the United States, traditional Italian Byzantine smalti are available from:
LEO POPPER AND SONS, INC: 143-147 Franklin Street, New York, N.Y. 10013
They will supply detailed information about materials and prices on request.
A $1\frac{1}{2}$-lb sample bag containing tiles of each of the colours they have in stock is obtainable.

LATCO PRODUCTS: 3371 Glendale Boulevard, Los Angeles 39, California
can supply Byzantine smalti, mirotile, crushed gems, and transparent
and opaque Venetian glass mosaic, and will send information, discount
prices and sample boards on request.

Smalti can be imported direct from Italy (allow about 4 to 5 weeks) from:

MELLONI AND MORETTI: Murano, Fond. Cavour 17

ANGELO ORSONI: Venezia (418), S. Giobbe 1045
Smalti import by freight is only worth while if you can order a fairly large
quantity at a time. For smaller amounts ask for despatch by post.

VITREOUS GLASS MOSAIC

Prices are usually quoted by the square foot. $1\frac{1}{2}$ to 2 lb will cover one square
foot and prices vary according to colour. For quantities above a certain
amount reductions are usually given.

Italian vitreous tesserae

EDGAR UDNY AND CO (see above)

DESIGN CRAFT MOSAICS: Christchurch Road, Ilford, Essex

MICHEL AND POLGAR LTD: 41 Blandford Street, London W 1

Swedish, Portuguese and Turkish Tesserae (of similar quality)

PROCTOR AND LAVENDER MOSAICS LTD: Solihull, Warwickshire
The most popular size of vitreous glass mosaic is $\frac{3}{4}$ in. by $\frac{3}{4}$ in. but a
variety of larger sizes are available at a somewhat higher cost.
Prices range in decreasing order according to colour groups.
Reds
Oranges
Yellows
Black
Greens, Blues, Turquoises, White, Greys, Browns

Glass and glazed porcelain tile mosaics are available in the United States from:

DILLON TILE SUPPLY COMPANY: 252-12th Street, San Francisco 3, California

F. E. BIEGERT CO, INC: 4801 Lemmon Avenue, Dallas, Texas

LATCO PRODUCTS (see above)

Detailed information about prices and materials is available on request.
Vitreous glass mosaics are sold either loose or mounted on sheets of
paper so that a whole sheet can be embedded into the mortar or adhesive.

CERAMIC TILES

Commercial Ceramic Tiles

$4\frac{1}{4}$ in. by $4\frac{1}{4}$ in. square and 6 in. by 6 in. square. Obtainable from local tile
or builders' merchants. A good range of 80 colours is made by:

CARTER TILES LTD: Poole, Dorset and 157 Clapham Road, London SW 9

Frost-proof Tiles
CARTER TILES LTD

Hand-made Tiles From stock or to order
PACKARD AND ORD: 37 Store Street, London WC 1

Small Ceramic Mosaic
The tesserae are similar in size to the vitreous glass tesserae, but their colours are restricted to about a dozen pastel shades and black and white. Suppliers:
EDGAR UDNY AND CO: PROCTOR AND LAVENDER: CARTER TILES LTD (see above)

   In the United States:

DILLON TILE SUPPLY COMPANY: F. E. BIEGERT CO INC: LATCO PRODUCTS (see above)

General Information about Ceramic Tiles and tiling
BRITISH CERAMIC TILE COUNCIL: Federation House, Stoke-on-Trent, Staffs

MARBLE

Polished marble scraps from local monumental masons. 1 cwt bags of unpolished marble in eight different shades from EDGAR UDNY AND CO.

ELDER REED AND CO LTD: 105 Battersea High Street, London SW 11

SLATE

From local builders' merchants or
JOHN WILLIAMS AND CO: 167 Rotherhithe Street, London SE 16

TOOLS

Spring-type cutters (Fig. 3) **and Japanese mosaic nippers** (Fig. 4):
EDGAR UDNY AND CO: MICHEL AND POLGAR LTD (see above)

Glass cutters and tile cutters (Figs. 5 and 6):
From local ironmongers

Surgical blades and holders (Fig. 7):
Swann-Morton No 23, made by
W. R. SWANN AND CO: Penn Works, Sheffield 6
Obtainable at Artists' Materials shops or
JOHN BELL AND CROYDEN: 50 Wigmore Street, London W 1

Stanley knives and blades (Fig. 8):
From ironmongers and Artists' Materials shops
General suppliers of tools, grout and mastics in the United States are:
DILLON TILE SUPPLY COMPANY: LATCO PRODUCTS: F. E. BIEGERT CO INC (see above)
GAGER'S HANDICRAFT: 1024 Nicollet Avenue, Minneapolis 3, Minnesota

CERAMIC MATERIALS AND GLAZES

TIRANTI LTD: 72 Charlotte Street, London W 1

WENGERS LTD: Etruria, Stoke-on-Trent, Staffs

They publish a comprehensive catalogue of lustres, enamels, glass colours, oxides, etc.

STAINED AND 'ANTIQUE' GLASS

MILLER, BEALE AND HIDER LTD: 162 Camden High Street, London NW 1

JAMES HETLEY AND CO LTD: Beresford Avenue, Wembley, Middlesex
Prices vary according to colours.

CEMENT COLOUR

Cementone, made by:

JOSEPH FREEMAN, SONS AND CO LTD: 96 Garrett Lane, London SW 18
Obtainable through leading builders' merchants.

PIGMENT (In powder form)

JOHN T. KEEP AND SONS LTD: 15 Theobald's Road, London WC 1

ADHESIVES AND MASTICS

PVA-based glues are available under a variety of trade names from hardware shops. *Uhu* has excellent glass-bonding power. *Bostik* is a rubber-based adhesive available in off-white and black.

A plastic emulsion adhesive is made in Italy specially for fixing glass tesserae, but can be used for fixing practically any other mosaic material to any type of base. The white water-based emulsion is non-inflammable and very clean to work with, since it can be washed off with water before it has set. It should be used for indoor mosaics only, since it is not waterproof. It dries completely transparent and is therefore particularly suitable for delicate work, since the adhesive in the crevices between tesserae is almost invisible. It is called *Lattix Cement* and must be imported from Italy from the manufacturers.

I recommend it especially to the professional mosaicist, who will find the extra trouble of importing it worth his while, since it is such an agreeable adhesive to work with. Any excess *Lattix Cement* between tesserae can be cut off with a surgical knife (Fig. 7) after it has dried.

L.A.C.I., Trezzano S/N (MI). Via Brunelleschi, Quartiere Zingone.

One of the strongest adhesives on the market is *Araldite* epoxy adhesive. It dries transparent and is suitable for all mosaic work and particularly for transparent glass mosaic windows. It is available from the manufacturers, CIBA (A.R.L.) Duxford, Cambridge. Various types of *Araldite* are being made. It is an epoxy resin which has to be mixed with a hardener immediately before use. *Araldite AY* 103 and *Hardener HY* 951 are to be mixed according to the manufacturers' Instruction Sheet. It is available in quantities from 1lb upwards. Mix the *Araldite* in a polythene container and protect your skin with a barrier cream or rubber gloves. At room temperature mix no more compound than you can use within approximately three hours, since the hardening process of *Araldite*, once started, cannot be reversed.

Fixite is a mosaic adhesive available from EDGAR UDNY AND CO. It is not waterproof and grouting is necessary. Waterproof *Fixite* grout is a powder which has to be mixed with water. It is essential that the mosaic base material is water-sealed before *Fixite* is applied.

A white plasticized adhesive cement is made by:

BUILDING ADHESIVES LTD: Federation House, Stoke-on-Trent, Staffs

and sold under the name of *CTF*. I have found its adhesive properties excellent. It is supplied in powder form and has to be mixed with water. *CTF* 1 is suitable for indoor use only, whereas *CTF* 2 is waterproof and can be used for outdoor mosaics. It will dry in about twenty minutes and therefore only small quantities should be mixed at one time. It can be used directly on a concrete base or brick wall, and its general application and suitability are similar to those of ordinary cement mortar as described in Chapter 6.

Richafix is another product of Building Adhesives Ltd; *Richafix* GREEN SEAL is a ready-mixed adhesive which is suitable for indoor use on all surfaces, including wood. *Richafix* RED SEAL is a waterproof grade which can be used for outdoor mosaics on any but painted surfaces. Their *Bal-Flex* adhesive is a grey plastic powder and liquid which have to be mixed. It is suitable for outdoor use and can be applied wherever cement mortar is applied; its main advantage over cement mortar is its very light weight. It is suitable for relief effects since it can be applied to any thickness.

Supplied by:

COPE AND CO LTD: 8 Gray's Inn Road, London WC 1

CARTER AND CO LTD: 157 Clapham Road, London SW 9

CTF adhesives are not normally stocked by suppliers, but information about local supplies can be obtained from the manufacturers.

Unibond is a good general adhesive for use on wood, concrete, etc. It is a suitable bonding agent for mixing with cement. Detailed instructions are supplied with the product.

Available at hardware stores and from EDGAR UDNY AND CO.

Manufactured by LIQUITILE SUPPLY CO LTD, 48 High Street, Camberley, Surrey.

Polybond is a plastic bonding agent available at hardware stores and builders' merchants. (Manufactured by POLYBOND LTD, Southampton.)

GLASS PLASTICS

Polyester Resin and Liquid Hardener,
Polyester Solvent (for cleaning purposes):

TIRANTI: 72 Charlotte Street, London W 1

Bondaglass CR 1 *Resin and Catalyst:*

BONDAGLASS LTD: 53-55 South End, Croydon, Surrey

Araldite Epoxy Resin AY 103 and *Hardener HY* 951

CIBA (A.R.L.) Duxford, Cambridge.

Epoxy Cleaning Liquid: any strong paint stripper.

Glass Fibre (by the yard), from

BONDAGLASS LTD: TIRANTI (see above)

PHOTOSTATS

REPHOTO CO LTD: IA Kempsford Road, London SE 11

CARDBOARD BOXES

For storing smalti and vitreous glass mosaic,

F. G. KETTLE: 127 High Holborn, London WC 1

METAL TABLE FRAMES *(for mosaic-topped tables)*

MICHEL AND POLGAR LTD (see above)

PERSPEX

MICHEL AND POLGAR LTD (see above)

General suppliers of mosaic materials

In South Africa:

MURANO GLASS WORKS LTD: 23-25 Fountain Road, Edenvale, Transvaal

In Canada:

BELL RINFRET ET CO.: 368 Notre Dame Ouest, Montreal, P.Q.

FRONTENAC LTD: 5150 Jean Talon W., Montreal, P.Q.

and at 1425 Bayview, Toronto, Ontario

Bibliography

Masterpieces of Greek Art
  Raymond V. Schoder. London: Studio Books. New York: N.Y. Graphic
Greek Painting
  Pierre Devambez. London: Weidenfeld & Nicolson. New York: The Viking Press
Roman Painting
  Amedea Mairui. London and New York: Skira World Publications
Roman and Etruscan Painting
  Arturo Stenico. London: Weidenfeld & Nicolson. New York: The Viking Press, Compass
    paperback
Byzantine Painting
  André Grabar. London and New York: Skira World Publications
Byzantine Art
  David Talbot Rice. London and Baltimore: Penguin Books, Pelican paperback
Byzantine Mosaic Decoration
  Otto Demus. London: Routledge, Kegan, Paul. Boston: Boston Book
A Concise History of Modern Painting
  Herbert Read. London: Thames & Hudson. New York: Frederick A. Praeger
European Painting and Sculpture
  Eric Newton. London and Baltimore: Penguin Books, Pelican paperback
Georges Pierre Seurat
  Reginald Howard Wilenski. London: Faber & Faber
Léger
  Katharine Kuh. Urbana, Illinois: University of Illinois Press
Antoni Gaudí
  James Johnson Sweeney and Josep Lluis Sert. London: Architectural Press. New York:
    Frederick A. Praeger
Outline of European Architecture
  Nikolaus Pevsner. London and Baltimore: Penguin Books, Jubilee edition and Pelican
    paperback
Guide to Modern Architecture
  Reyner Banham. London: Architectural Press. New York: D. Van Nostrand
Introduction to Modern Architecture
  J. M. Richards. London and Baltimore: Penguin Books, Pelican paperback
'My Work'
  Le Corbusier (pseudonym). Translated by James Palmes. London: Architectural Press
The New Architecture and The Bauhaus
  Walter Gropius. London: Faber & Faber. Newton Centre, Massachusetts: Charles T.
    Branford
Art in European Architecture
  Paul Damaz. New York: Reinhold
Art in Latin American Architecture
  Paul Damaz. New York: Reinhold
Art in Modern Architecture
  Eleanor Bittermann. New York: Reinhold
How to Make Collages
  John Lynch. London: Thames & Hudson. New York: The Viking Press
The Art of Making Mosaics
  Louisa Jenkins and Barbara Mills. New York: D. Van Nostrand
Mosaics of Jeanne Reynal
  Jeanne Reynal. Edited by Dore Ashton and others. New York: George Wittenborn
Practical Pottery and Ceramics
  Kenneth Clark. London: Studio Vista. New York: The Viking Press
The Complete Book of Artist's Techniques
  Kurt Herberts. London: Thames & Hudson. New York: Frederick A. Praeger
Vasari on Technique
  Giorgio Vasari. Edited by B. Baldwin Brown. London: J. M. Dent. New York: Dover
    Publications, paperback
Glass Fibre for Amateurs
  G. M. Lewis and R. H. Warring. London: Model Aeronautical Press
Glass in Architecture and Decoration
  Raymond McGrath and A. C. Frost. London: Architectural Press
The Artist's Handbook of Materials and Techniques
  Ralph Mayer. London: Faber & Faber

Index